99 Things You Wish You Knew

Before®... Your Identity

Was Stolen

Your guide to protecting yourself from
identity theft and computer fraud

Robert Siciliano

www.99-series.com

The 99 Series
85 N. Main Street
Florida, NY 10921
646-233-4366

The author has done his/her best to present accurate and up-to-
date information in this book, but he/she cannot guarantee that the
information is correct or will suit your particular situation.

This book is sold with the understanding that the publisher and the
author are not engaged in rendering any legal, accounting or any
other professional services. If expert assistance is required, the
services of a competent professional should be sought.

First published by The 99 Series 2011

Ginger Marks Cover designed and Layout
DocUmeantDesigns www.DocUmeantDesigns.com

Caitlin Podiak Copy Editor
http://caitlinpodiak.tumblr.com/contact

Distributed by DocUmeant Publishing

For inquiries about volume orders, please contact:**99 Book
Series, Inc.**
books@99-series.com

**Library of Congress Cataloging-in-Publication Data
Siciliano, Robert**
        **99 Things You Wish You Knew Before Your
Identity Was Stolen: identity theft, computer fraud,
crime, prevention.**

LCCN - 2011940660

Printed in the United States Of America
ISBN-13: 978-0-9832122-9-4 (paperback)
ISBN-10: 0983212295

Stay Safe Online

McAfee Total Protection

The most effective protection against virus, online and network threats.

~~$89.99~~
$44.99
Save $45.00

Buy Now!

- Protect against viruses and malware
- Block spam and dangerous email
- Protect your personal data
- Protect against hackers and thieves
- Protect your identity
- Protect your social network

http://home.mcafee.com/root/campaign.aspx?cid=89163

DEDICATION

This book is dedicated to anyone who has been a victim of any kind of crime. It is for you that we, as security professionals, do what we do.

CONTENTS

CHAPTER 6

CHAPTER 7

ABOUT THE 99 SERIES

The 99 Series is a collection of quick, easy-to-understand guides that spell it all out for you in the simplest format; 99 points, one lesson per page. The book series is the one-stop shop for all readers tired of looking all over for self-help books. The 99 Series brings it all to you under one umbrella! The bullet point format that is the basis for all the 99 Series books was created purposely for today's fast-paced society. Not only does information have to be at our finger tips … we need it quickly and accurately without having to do much research to find it. But don't be fooled by the easy-to-read format. Each of the books in the series contains very thorough discussions from our roster of professional authors so that all the information you need to know is compiled into one book!

We hope that you will enjoy this book as well as the rest of the series. If you've enjoyed our books, tell your friends. And if you feel we need to improve something, please feel free to give us your feedback at www.99-series.com.

Helen Georgaklis
Founder & CEO, 99 Series

PREFACE

As the Internet grows ever more pervasive and essential, we find ourselves conducting most of our business online. We use the Internet to shop, pay bills, and manage bank accounts. We will increasingly rely on the electronic exchange of personal information as the Internet continues to evolve and become even more consumer friendly. Subsequently, criminals will also evolve, working day and night to find and exploit vulnerabilities within our networks. These hackers will not sleep until they gain access to all of our information, which they can utilize to steal our identities or gain access to our financial accounts.

I once believed that I had taken all the necessary precautions to protect my small business. I shared the misconception that a criminal would never target me. But as I learned, and as most individuals will soon learn, identity theft and financial loss due to criminal activity happen more often than we realize. Statistics show that one in four American adults have been notified by a business or organization that their information has been compromised due to a data breach. This means that you could be taking all the necessary precautions to keep your information safe, but by simply doing what every other person in the world does—sharing your Social Security Number or credit card information with a trusted organization—you have put yourself and your security at risk. So, how do you protect yourself?

Having been entrenched in the field of personal security for the past 20 years, I have kept up with the latest technological advances and shared my expertise. I am often called upon to comment in all areas of media, including the Internet, television, newspapers, and magazines. Through blogs, articles, and interviews, I have offered advice on how individuals, as well as businesses, need to do in order to protect themselves from criminals. There always has been and always will be criminals seeking their next victim. Your job is to put up defenses so they don't choose you. This book will help you to put systems into place to thwart a criminal from determining you are the next target.

ACKNOWLEDGMENTS

This book would not be possible without the help and support of my great clients.

Security companies, while they are for-profit businesses, always have their clients' most precious needs in mind. We in the security business are the good fighting against evil. We deal with the worst of human predators and the people they victimize on a daily basis.

Fortunately, there are great companies like McAfee, Inc. who employ thousands of people globally to work 24/7 to fight the good fight. It is my honor to serve with true professionals on the McAfee® Consumer Advisory Board and to work with McAfee to keep consumers safe and secure.

INTRODUCTION

My first exposure to personal security occurred at a young age when I became a target for the neighborhood bully. Due to the constant attacks, I became interested in the art of self-preservation. While most of my classmates were mastering things like sports and academics, I concentrated on finding ways to stay safe. This led me to enroll in a number of different self-defense classes.

In the process of learning to defend myself, I met a young woman who had been sexually assaulted. I was too young to know what sex was, let alone rape. It was a foreign concept to me. Nevertheless, I clearly understood what it was like to be the target of an attack. As time passed, I began to meet other young girls who had been attacked in the same way. Consequently, my focus turned toward personal security—not just for myself, but also for those around me.

I grew older and security became more than just violence prevention; it included theft prevention as well. When the Internet gained popularity, security meant information security and identity theft protection. As the need for information and identity security increased, my focus expanded to include these areas.

These new types of crimes affected me personally in the mid-1990s. At that time, I had a small business with a dial-up connection to the Internet. In order to conduct business and accept payments from clients, I had obtained the technology that allowed me to accept credit cards. Unfortunately, within a week of opening my doors, the computer I used to run my small business was hacked, and fraudulent orders were placed with stolen credit card information. A lot of money was lost, and as the vendor, I was held responsible for what happened.

Around the same time, a good friend of the family had her identity stolen. Because I had experience going through my own ordeal, I worked with my friend to investigate who had stolen her identity. After doing some research, we determined that her mail had been stolen from her mailbox and that the perpetrator was a woman from a suburb of Boston, who had 45 prior convictions for fraud. When we uncovered her identity and sordid past, we turned the information over to the authorities, who promptly arrested her. She was eventually prosecuted, but only received a one-year suspended sentence. This was a slap on the wrist compared to the loss my friend suffered. Back then, the punishment for theft identity definitely did not fit the crime. When I saw how easy it was for this criminal to steal my friend's mail and open accounts using her identity, and only receive a slap on the wrist, I thought to myself that identity theft would soon become an enormous problem ... and it has.

After being victimized by this type of crime, I have had the opportunity to work with thousands of other victims, as well as people who, like me, have made it their job to protect unsuspecting citizens. Being in the trenches for as long as I have—since this type of crime took root—I developed a keen ability to identify likely victims and perpetrators, and I also learned the many ins and outs of how these crimes are committed. For the past 20 years, I have been writing, speaking, and consulting on the issue of

identify theft and have worked with highly respected security companies to help consumers
protect themselves from attacks.

Throughout the pages of this book, you will
learn the tricks of the trade in an easy-to-understand format. After reading this book you will
have the tools and the knowledge to defend
yourself from the omnipresent bullies who have
made their living dipping into the pockets of
everyday people like you and me.

PART ONE: IDENTITY THEFT BASICS

CHAPTER 1

WHAT IS IDENTITY THEFT?

Identity theft occurs when someone takes your personally identifiable information (PII), and misuses it, abuses it, and adapts it to his or her own life, often for financial gain. When an identity thief does this, your good name is soiled—the name you have worked so hard to keep in good standing. Rectifying it can be as simple as a phone call, or it can be as difficult as having to prove your innocence to a jury of your peers.

Identity theft, also known as identity fraud, encompasses various types of crimes. The identifying factor is that a criminal has wrongfully acquired and adopted someone else's personal data. This can include the victim's name, Social

Security Number, address, date of birth, credit card information, bank account number, or any other type of personal information.[1]

When identity theft affects you, it can consume your time and ruin your credit. You become a liability for an employer or a college administrator. You may be perceived as someone who has bad credit as a result of your own doing. You have a black mark on your reputation. In short, it is the victims, not the criminals, who have a difficult time functioning in a credit-driven society.

What follows is a real-world example of this type of crime:

An 18-year-old man was driving in his vehicle, and he rolled through a stop sign. He was pulled over by a police officer who witnessed the offense. When the police officer checked his information, it was determined that there was a warrant out for his arrest for numerous prior violations. After his arrest and subsequent trip to the police station, they learned that his Social

---

[1] For more information, see Robert Siciliano, "What Exactly Is Identity Theft?," Scottrade Community, *Identity Theft Insights* (blog), October 27, 2010, http://community.scottrade.com/blogs/981/2230.

Security Number was tied to a man who was 49 years old. This young man learned that his identity had been stolen a number of years ago! The identity thief had opened up several businesses in the young man's name while he was still a child. Identity theft is the only crime that I am aware of in which you are presumed guilty until proven innocent.

#1: What Are the Categories that Define Identity Theft?

There are six basic categories of identity theft:

1. New Account Fraud
2. Account Takeover Fraud
3. Criminal Identity Theft
4. Identity Cloning
5. Medical Identity Theft
6. Business or Commercial Identity Theft

These categories will be explained in detail in later chapters. As I have witnessed throughout the many years I have worked with victims, each type of identity theft can have a devastating impact. Victims with whom I have worked with are taxpaying citizens who do the right thing, who work hard to earn honest livings. When their personal information was compromised, thieves opened up financial accounts in their victims' names, and when these new accounts were opened, it affected the victims' ability to rent an apartment, buy a car, or buy a home. When your good name is stolen and stained, you are thrown into a position where you are responsible for fixing it. This means you are delayed in getting the car, home, or apartment you need. For those seeking employment, it also means you could lose the opportunity to get a job, because some employers check credit scores to learn more about prospective hires.

#2: How Common Is Identity Theft?

Identity theft in the form of new account fraud can happen to anyone with a Social Security Number, which includes virtually anyone with a pulse, as well as some who are dead. Identity theft can even happen to a newborn baby shortly after a Social Security Number has been issued to that child.

Within days of a child's birth, the proud parents typically sign documentation prior to being released from the hospital, and a Social Security Number is issued within a few weeks. That number is promptly distributed to many entities:

the U.S. Social Security Administration has it; the hospital has it; doctors' offices have it; the newborn's insurance company has it; the Internal Revenue Service (IRS) has it—everybody with access to these documents and computer files has access to it.

When the child goes to school and joins various sporting teams and church groups, his or her Social Security Number is distributed even wider. As the child ages and gets a driver's license, a first job, or attends college, the number continues to be shared. Anyone who has access to the relevant documents or files can also gain access to that person's identity.

Throughout adulthood, he or she will get mortgages and credit cards and change jobs, and the Social Security Number will be distributed to an even wider net. In the end, after this person dies and an obituary is printed, identity thieves can still use his or her Social Security Number. Even in death you are not protected from identity theft!

#3: What Are the Latest Identity Theft Statistics?

Here are some eye-opening statistics from McAfee:[2]

- $54 billion—the amount Americans incurred in loss from identity theft in 2008[3]
- 500 million—the number of consumers from 2005 to 2009 whose personal and financial data has been exposed as a result of corporate data breaches—events the victims cannot control despite taking personal safety measures[4]

---

[2] "Theft Statistics," McAfee Identity Protection: Counter Identity Theft Unit, accessed May 12, 2011.

[3] "2010 Identity Fraud Survey Report," Javelin Strategy & Research, February 2010, https://www.javelinstrategy.com/research/Brochure-170.

[4] Identity Theft Info, n.d., http://identitytheftinfo.com.

- $5,000—the average fraud amount per victim[5]
- 400%—victims who found out about their identity theft more than six months after it happened incurred costs four times higher than the average
- 165 hours—the average amount of time victims spent repairing the damage done by creation of new fraudulent accounts[6]
- 89%—the percentage of personal identity thefts that take place offline[7]
- 58 hours—the average amount of time victims spent repairing the damage done to existing accounts[8]
- 43%—the percentage of identity theft occurring from stolen wallets, checkbooks, credit cards, billing statements, or other physical documents

---

[5] "2009 Identity Fraud Survey Report," Javelin Strategy & Research, February 2009, https://www.javelinstrategy.com/Brochure/114.

[6] Identity Theft Research Center. Identity Theft: The Aftermath 2008

[7] "2009 Identity Fraud Survey Report," Javelin.

[8] "Aftermath 2008," Identity Theft Resource Center.

- 1 in 4—number of American adults who have been notified by a business or checkbooks, credit cards, billing statements, or other physical documents
- 1 in 4—number of American adults who have been notified by a business or organization that their information has been compromised due to a data breach[9]
- 11%—the percentage of personal identities stolen using the Internet[10]
- Once every three seconds—how often an identity is stolen[11]

#4: What Are the Warning Signs of Identity Theft?

People often discover that their identity has been stolen when they are denied credit. So when you apply for a loan to purchase a car or a home, and you are denied credit, you may discover that it is a result of your credit being damaged by fraud. Accounts may have been opened without your

---

[9] "2010 Identity Fraud Survey Report," Javelin.

[10] "2009 Identity Fraud Survey Report," Javelin.

[11] "2010 Identity Fraud Survey Report," Javelin.

authorization, and the resulting bills would never have been paid.

#5: Can Identity Theft Interfere with My Ability to Get a Job or Obtain Credit?

Some people learn that their identity has been stolen when they are denied employment. An employer may check an applicant's credit history to determine whether he or she is financially responsible. If the applicant's identity has been stolen, assuming the thief hasn't been surreptitiously paying the bills, the employer rejects the applicant based on a credit history tainted by fraud. Schools may also deny admission after checking a prospective student's credit history, or the student may be unable to secure a college loan because an identity thief has opened accounts in the student's name. Parents may also discover their identities have been stolen when they apply for loans to pay for their children's tuition and are denied. Debt collectors may even call identity theft victims, demanding payment for goods or services that the victims never purchased or received. In a worst-case scenario, a victim is arrested for a crime he or she did not commit.

#6: What Does the Government Say About Identity Theft?

The Federal Trade Commission (FTC) provides the following list of warning signs that your identity may have been stolen[12]:

- Accounts you didn't open and debts on your accounts that you can't explain
- Fraudulent or inaccurate information on your credit reports, including accounts and personal information, such as your Social Security Number, address, name or initials, or employer
- Failing to receive bills or other mail (this could indicate that an identity thief has taken over your account and changed your billing address—follow up with creditors if your bills don't arrive on time)
- Receiving credit cards that you didn't apply for

---

[12] "Detect Identity Theft," Fighting Back Against Identity Theft: Federal Trade Commission, accessed May 12, 2011,
http://www.ftc.gov/bcp/edu/microsites/idtheft/consumers/detect.html#Whatarethesignsofidentitytheft.

- Being denied credit or being offered less favorable credit terms, like a high interest rate, for no apparent reason
- Getting calls or letters from debt collectors or businesses about merchandise or services you didn't buy

#7: What Are the Warning Signs of Child Identity Theft?

Since children can also be victims of identity theft, a call from a bill collector informing you that your two-year-old bought a Mercedes and defaulted on the loan would be a major warning sign. Or perhaps law enforcement may come knocking on your door to inquire about crimes committed by your newborn child.

There have also been instances in which parents registering their child for school find out that another child in the school has the same name and Social Security Number. This often occurs in cases where the other child is an illegal alien. Some studies have shown that for someone who is a victim of illegal alien identity theft, his or her Social Security Number is shared an average of thirty times. There are 12 million illegal aliens in the U.S., and some will buy, sell, or steal a legal citizen's Social Security Number in order to live and work in America.

#8: How Does Identity Theft Affect My Life?

Identity theft victims suffer losses of time, as well as money. Studies show that identity theft can take anywhere from one hour to 600 hours to rectify, which can potentially add up to several years of your life. Other studies have shown that as many as one out of four victims never fully restore their compromised identities. They have to deal with it for the rest of their lives. It's just a constant administrative process that never goes away.

A child whose identity has been stolen often has difficulty getting a start in our credit-driven society. The child may be denied a credit card, a college or car loan, or a job.

For some people, the consequences of identity theft include financial ruin, wrecked marriages, lost jobs, or emotional distress. It can be like a recurring cancer. Identity theft is not something you want to happen to you or anyone you love.

#9: What Are the Two Most Common Ways Identities Are Stolen?

Criminals can steal your identity by going through your trash, by stealing your mail, or by breaking into your house and rifling through your file cabinets. All they need is a sheet of paper with your name and a few personal details.

Criminals also steal identities via the Internet. One method is to hack into a database containing Social Security Numbers, along with passwords and account numbers.

Some studies have shown that as much as 70 percent of identity theft is committed from the inside, meaning that the thief has direct access to the victim's personal data. The person on the inside could be a Director of Human Resources, or their assistant, or anyone who has access to filing cabinets and databases containing employee information. Employees can be involved in identity theft in other ways. Every time you hand over your credit card at a gas station or a grocery store, or give out the number over the Internet or phone, you are directly or indirectly providing your credit card number to someone who is fully capable of stealing it. Any credit card number can be copied and used to make purchases online or over the phone, or to create a cloned credit card, which can be used in stores.

CHAPTER 2

WHO STEALS IDENTITIES?

Identity thieves often have personal connections to their victims. They could be friends or family members, employees or employers. Or they could be complete strangers who simply went through your trash or stole your mail, or criminal hackers in a foreign country.

What drives the thieves to commit these heinous crimes? Perpetrators of identity theft are typically driven by desperation, mental illness, or unusual greed. Some, however, are organized criminals who will do whatever it takes to poach someone else's money.

Hackers all over the world utilize sophisticated hacking tools to access databases that house our private information. In particular, they are after the following data:

- Social Security Numbers
- Credit card numbers
- Bank account information
- Home and business addresses
- Birth dates

These criminals break into networks that store these valuable numbers, steal the data, and use it to take over our existing accounts. In a single night, they can make charges to our credit cards, initiate electronic funds transfers, and deplete our accounts, all before we even get out of bed the next day.

What follows is a recap of the antics of one of the most notorious cybercriminals known to man:

Albert Gonzalez, the son of a Cuban immigrant, began his reign of terror before he was old enough to drive. He became fascinated with computer viruses at the age of 12, when his new computer was infected with a virus. Through the process of learning how to protect his equipment from future invasions, he also learned how to profit from them.

A recent New York Times article (James Verini, 2010)[13] depicts this young man's whirlwind career as one of the most prolific cybercriminals on record. By the age of 14, Gonzalez was using stolen account information to order merchandise online. He had his ill-gotten purchases delivered to empty houses, from which he would retrieve the products during his lunch break. After he hacked into NASA servers, FBI agents visited Gonzalez at his school, but that did not slow him down. At 22, he was arrested at an ATM in Upper Manhattan, sporting a fake nose ring and a woman's wig, using multiple debit cards he had created with stolen account information. Police soon realized what a catch Gonzalez was: he was a well-respected leader in a cyber gang.

After his arrest, authorities convinced Gonzalez to help take down the rest of his gang. Even those who worked closely with

---

[13] James Verini, "The Great Cyberheist," *New York Times*, November 10, 2010, http://www.nytimes.com/2010/11/14/magazine/14Hacker-t.html?src=tp.

him failed to realize that Gonzalez was a double agent of sorts. While helping detectives work against online victimization, Gonzalez continued stealing with a tight-knit crew of hackers. Gonzalez's group pulled off such crimes as hacking into 7-Eleven's network of ATMs.

In the end, he received two consecutive 20-year prison terms for stealing information that gave him access to 180 million credit and debit card accounts at stores including OfficeMax, Target, JC Penney, and many more.

#10: How Has Hacking Evolved with Technological Advances?

In the late '90s and early 2000s, hacking had evolved from "phreaking" (hacking phone systems) to "cracking" (breaking into networks). The early hackers were innovative individuals who wanted to understand the nature of telephone systems, and they used very simple tools to overcome those systems.

Over the years, as technology evolved and personal computers were born, these same hackers began to use newly available technological tools to share information with one another. As more government agencies and corporations adopted these same tools and technologies, the hackers started tinkering with the evolving systems and discovered vulnerabilities within the framework.

At first, they made the organizations that they had hacked into aware of their systems' vulnerabilities. Companies still took offense to these intrusions, and soon, laws were passed to make this type of hacking illegal. But hacking isn't something that a hacker can repress. It's in their blood. Therefore, they continue to hack.

Some hack nefariously; for them it's all about the thrill. They enjoy the challenge of breaking into systems and causing problems by deleting files or scrolling something obscene across a computer's desktop. They may even crash a system. When their hacking peers find out about what they have done, they become pseudo-famous overnight among other hackers. Fame and popularity within the hacking community are what started it all.

As we began spending more time shopping, banking, and managing personal affairs online, hackers abandoned their quests for fun and fame in order to realize a financial gain. Hackers are no longer deleting files, tormenting IT administrators, or wreaking havoc for its own sake. Now, they're stealing proprietary data for illegal profits.

#11: Is Hacking Good or Bad?

Hacking—in the context that we are discussing in this book—is ultimately bad. Hacking means undeserved and illegal financial gain at the expense of others. When it occurs, it results in substantial financial damages for the government, major corporations, and individuals whose identities have been stolen.

It is important to understand that "hacking" is not inherently a bad word. Over the past fifteen years, it has been become associated with identity theft and other crimes. Purists in the hacking community will often refer to the bad kind of hacking as "cracking."

Generally, hackers are both good and bad. They are technologically savvy individuals who are usually a head above the rest when it comes to the technology that is at our fingertips every day. Some hack for fun, while others hack for financial gain—the latter are the bad hackers.

#12: How Do I Distinguish the Good Hackers from the Bad?

There are seven types of hackers. Some are good and some are bad:

- **White hat hackers:** These are the good guys—computer security experts who specialize in penetration testing and other methodologies to ensure that a company's information systems are secure. These IT security professionals rely on a constantly evolving arsenal of technology to battle hackers. Sometimes, criminal hackers who are caught and rehabilitated go on to help to strengthen security systems from an attack. But recall the story of Albert Gonzalez—one can never be sure which side a once-criminal hacker is on.

- **Black hat hackers:** These are the bad guys, who are typically referred to simply as "hackers." The term "black hat hackers" is used specifically for hackers who break into networks or individual computers, or for hackers who create computer viruses. Black hat hackers tend to technologically outpace white hats. They always seem to find the path of least resistance, whether due to human error or laziness, or by employing a new type of attack. As previously mentioned, hacking purists often use the term "crackers" to refer to black hat hackers. A black hats hacker's motivation is to get paid.

- **Script kiddies:** This is a derogatory term for black hat hackers who attempt to make names for themselves by using borrowed programs to attack networks and deface websites.

- **Hacktivists:** Some hackers are activists motivated by politics or religion, while others may wish to expose wrongdoing, exact revenge, or simply harass their target for their own entertainment.

- **State-sponsored hackers:** Governments around the globe realize that it serves their military objectives to be well-positioned online. The saying used to be, "He who controls the seas controls the world." And then it was, "He who controls the air controls the world." Now it's all about controlling cyberspace. State-sponsored hackers have limitless time and funding to target civilians, corporations, and governments.

- **Spy hackers:** Corporations hire hackers to infiltrate the competition and steal trade secrets. A spy hacker may hack into an organization's servers from the outside or gain employment in order to act as a mole. Spy hackers may use similar tactics as hacktivists, but their only agenda is to serve their client's goals and get paid.

- **Cyber terrorists:** These hackers are generally motivated by religious or political beliefs, but unlike hactivists they attempt to create fear and chaos by disrupting critical infrastructures. Cyber terrorists are by far the most dangerous, with a wide range of skills and goals. A cyber terrorist's ultimate motivation is to spread terror and even to commit murder.

#13: How Is Hacking Done?

Hackers use penetration-testing tools—a variety of different hardware and software used to seek out vulnerabilities within a network. The vulnerabilities may be in a target's Internet connection—wired or wireless—or they may be found in the operating system, especially if it does not have updated security patches. Hacking tools often look for vulnerabilities in Internet browsers. These penetration-testing tools are available to both white hat and black hat hackers.

Ten years ago, criminal hackers created viruses that compromised your machine by deleting your files or crashing your hard drive. Not anymore. Today, they want your computer running smoothly and efficiently. The latest viruses sit dormant on your hard drive until they are awakened by a signal from their operators. Many of these viruses are Trojans that are designed to detect when you are banking online. They sit and wait, until you log onto your banking system, and then they strike.

Our bodies contain numerous viruses that become active when our immune systems are down, or when a virus makes contact with another virus and "wakes up." Your computer is similar. There is often something harmful lurking, but it may not be active yet. Viruses can infect our computers when we unknowingly visit the wrong website, click the wrong link in an email, or download the wrong program. While these are the most common ways to contract a virus, there are many more. Studies show that the number of viruses has quadrupled over the past few years. The problem is that the technology used by criminal hackers has been evolving at a faster rate than the technology used by white hats.

#14: What Role Does Organized Crime Play in Identity Theft?

Organized crime used to be all about muscle. It was loan sharking, gambling, drugs, and prostitution. While that stereotype is still very much alive today, organized crime leaders have learned that it is just as easy, and often easier than their traditional criminal activity, to employ hackers to break into databases containing vast amounts of personal information, and to use that data to open up new accounts or take over existing accounts, while the victims remain completely unaware.

#15: What Is Cybercrime?

Cybercrime primarily refers to the electronic theft of data, such as individuals' personal identifying information, corporate trade secrets, or even state secrets. Cybercrime garnered mainstream awareness after criminal hackers started breaking into databases full of sensitive data and using that data to commit identity theft or espionage.

Cybercrime is one of the most lucrative illegal businesses of our time, and it shows no signs of slowing down. Over the last decade, cyber crooks have developed new and increasingly sophisticated ways of capitalizing on the explosion of Internet users, and they face little danger of being caught. Meanwhile, consumers are confronted with greater risks to their money and information each year.

#16: What Are the Most Notable Cybercrimes?

Here are a few examples of famous cybercrimes:

- **The "I Love You" worm's false affection ($15 billion estimated damage):** Emails with the subject line "I love you" proved irresistible in 2000. Millions of users downloaded an attached file, which was supposedly a love letter but turned out to be a virus. This infamous worm cost companies and government agencies big time.
- **MyDoom's mass infection ($38 billion estimated damage):** This fast-moving worm, which first struck in 2004, tops a

McAfee list in terms of monetary damage. It delivered enough spam to slow global Internet access by 10 percent and reduced access to some websites by 50 percent, costing billions of dollars in lost productivity and online sales.

- **Conficker's stealthy destruction ($9.1 billion estimated damage):** This 2008 worm infected millions of computers. It went a step further than the previous two worms on this list, downloading and installing a variety of malware that gave hackers remote control over victims' computers.

#17: Why Would Cybercriminals Go After Me?

A cybercriminal's goal is to steal your identity: your name, Social Security Number, date of birth, address, and any other identifying personal information. They're also looking for bank accounts, credit card accounts, or any type of data that they can use to open up new accounts or take over existing accounts, so they can ultimately get paid.

Over the past 70 years, the Social Security Number has become our de facto national identifier. The numbers were first issued in the 1930s to track income for Social Security benefits. But "functionality creep" (which occurs when an item, process, or procedure ends up serving a purpose that it was never intended to perform) soon took effect. Decades later, the Social Security Number has become the key to the kingdom. You're required to disclose your Social Security Number regularly, and it appears in hundreds—even thousands—of files, records, and databases, accessible to an untold number of people.

Anyone who has access your Social Security Number can use it to impersonate you in a hospital or bank, or they can use it to get a job or obtain credit.

#18: How Would Cybercriminals Go After Me?

Our information is stored in hundreds if not thousands of databases, from government agencies and corporations to your own computer. A cybercriminal can access that information by finding vulnerabilities in your network or any network that hosts your information.

If the wireless Internet connection in your home or office is not secure, you're vulnerable. If the operating system on your computer is not up to date, you're vulnerable. If the browser on your computer is outdated, you're vulnerable. If, while on your own computer, you visit risky websites or online gaming sites that are hosted in foreign countries, you're vulnerable. If you download pirated software, movies, or music, you're vulnerable. If you engage in illicit activities on the Internet, you're vulnerable. Even if all of your security software is updated, if you enter credit card information into a website that is not properly secured, you're vulnerable. If you enter your Social Security Number into a website that is not properly secured, you're vulnerable. If you provide your data to a company that believes they are fully secure, but whose employees might open phishing emails that can compromise their entire network, you're vulnerable.

Cybercriminals target anyone and everyone, whether their systems are secured or not, in order to obtain as much identifying personal information as possible.

Any organization that extends credit requires your name, address, date of birth, and Social Security Number in order to verify your identity and run a credit check. This includes hospitals, insurance companies, banks, credit card issuers, car dealerships and other retailers. Even video rental stores may opt to run a credit check before trusting you with a borrowed DVD.

Now more than ever before, criminal hackers are hacking into databases containing Social Security Numbers and using those numbers to open new financial accounts. Criminals can use stolen Social Security Numbers to obtain mobile phones, credit cards, or bank loans. Some victims whose Social Security Numbers fell into the hands of identity thieves have even had their mortgages refinanced without their knowledge, robbing them of the equity of their home.

Having no credit or poor credit, no money in savings, and a nearly empty checking account does not prevent you from being targeted by identity thieves. A Social Security Number alone can be used to obtain credit, even when the identity theft victim doesn't have a good credit history. There are institutions and businesses that will open up new credit accounts at high interest rates for those with bad credit. With your Social Security Number, an identity thief can open a bank account under your name and deposit the mandatory $100. That's all it takes to acquire a checkbook, which the thief can use to write a dozen checks within a day or two, buying almost anything at all from various retail stores, all in your name, and then turn around and sell it all for pure profit.

The technologies that we use every day have become an indispensable aspect of our lives. We rely on the Internet and our personal computers more than ever, and the ways of life that we used to know have already been changed forever. We will continue to be increasingly dependent upon technology. As this occurs, criminals will dedicate even more attention to finding a wider range of innovative ways to exploit technological tools compromise your security. While they seek out the vulnerabilities in networks both big and small—yours and mine—security professionals are doing anything and everything they can to protect us from the bad guys.

Nevertheless, it's up to each of us to protect our own identity. That might entail anything from shredding documentation, locking your mailbox, protecting your Social Security Number, or investing in identity theft protection, because the issue of cybercrime and identity theft is not going to get any better. Unfortunately, it will only get worse.

CHAPTER 3

TYPES OF IDENTITY THEFT

When most people think of identity theft, their credit cards are their first concern. Many people who have had their credit cards compromised believe they have been victims of identity theft. While credit card fraud is a form of identity theft, it is certainly not the most damaging. Credit card fraud is something that personal security professionals refer to as "account take-over." This occurs when someone takes over an existing account. Should your account be compromised, it is your responsibility to report any loss to the issuing bank within a set time period, usually 60 days, in order to have the lost funds restored to your account. When a credit card is compromised, the resolution usually takes no longer than a couple of months, and it is a single occurrence.

The most damaging form of identity theft occurs when a thief opens new in under your name. These accounts are linked to your Social Security Number and your credit history. In a credit-driven society in which creditors, employers, and insurers judge you solely based on credit scores, you may be looked upon negatively and even denied credit, employment, insurance, and other services as a result of having your identity stolen.

It's important to realize that identity theft can happen to groups of people, not just individuals. Credit card companies, banks, financial advisors, retailers, hospitals, insurance companies, and virtually every other industry and organization that deals with finances has been affected by large-scale identity theft and fraud. For some, it's an occasional nuisance. For others, it's the reality of doing business. Most have heavily invested in multiple layers of security, but all remain targets to some extent. Each business its own particular set of issues to overcome, but at the same time, each copes with the same underlying constant:

the consumer—their customer—is the most vulnerable variable in the equation.

Whether they realize it or not, most people offer the path of least resistance to scammers, whether they are leaving themselves vulnerable to phishing emails or spoofed websites, or by failing to adequately protect and update computers, leaving wireless connections open, being inattentive to bank statements, discarding documents without shredding them first, or carrying too much information in their wallets. Most people tend to overlook their own personal security, allowing fraud to flourish unchecked.

One identity theft victim serves as a tragic example of the potential consequences of this crime. 17 years ago, when Larry Smith was 50 years old, Joseph Kidd stole his identity. While operating under Smith's identity, Kidd was arrested, sent to prison, and eventually paroled. He later obtained welfare and Medicare benefits. He got married. He did all of this using Smith's name.

Smith had to deal with the imposter's actions from afar, just as if he himself had a criminal record, was married, and on welfare. Even though the real Smith has no criminal record, he spent eight days in jail because of Kidd's crimes. He also had liens placed on his home, was denied medical care, and lost his driver's license, all due to his identity being stolen.

When people ask, "Why would anyone steal my identity? I have no money," I point to Joseph Smith. When they say, "But I have bad credit," I point to Smith. When they say, "I don't have a computer or credit cards. I pay cash and I don't bank online," I point to Smith.

This is what identity theft looks like. It goes far beyond your computer being hacked or your credit card number being used without your permission. What happened to Larry Smith is identity theft.

#19: What Is Financial Identity Theft?

The FTC offers a comprehensive explanation of identity theft:

> *Identity theft occurs when someone uses the identifying information of another person— name, Social Security Number, mother's maiden name, or other personal information—to commit fraud or engage in other unlawful activities. For example, an identity*

thief may open up a new credit card account under someone else's name. When the identity thief fails to pay the bills, the bad debt is reported on the victim's credit report. Other common forms of identity theft include taking over an existing credit card account and making unauthorized charges on it. Typically, the identity thief forestalls discovery by the victim by contacting the credit-card issuer and changing the billing address on the account; taking out loans in another person's name; writing fraudulent checks using another person's name and/or account number; and using personal information to access, and transfer money out of, another person's bank or brokerage account. In extreme cases, the identity thief may completely take over his or her victim's identity—opening a bank account, getting multiple credit cards, buying a car, getting a home mortgage and even working under the victim's name.

Identity theft almost always involves a financial services institution in some way—as a lender, holder of a bank account, or credit card or debit card issuer—because, as the bank robber Willie Sutton observed, that is where the money is. Identity theft involving financial services institutions, furthermore, is accomplished through a wide variety of means. Historically, identity thieves have been able to get the personal information they need to operate through simple, "low-tech" methods: intercepting orders of new checks in the mail, for example, or rifling through the trash to get discarded bank account statements or pre-approved credit card offers. Sometimes, identity thieves will try to trick others into giving up this information. One way in which identity thieves do this is by "pretexting," or calling on false pretenses, such as by telephoning banks and posing as the account holder. In other cases, the identity thief may contact the victim directly. In one recent scheme, fraud artists have reportedly been preying on consumers' fears about Year 2000 computer bugs. A caller, for example, represents that he or she is from the consumer's bank and tells the consumer that the caller needs certain information about the consumer's account (or needs to transfer money to a special account) in order to ensure the bank can comply with Year 2000 requirements.

Other methods of identity theft may involve more sophisticated techniques. In a practice known as "skimming," identity thieves use computers to read and store the information encoded on the magnetic strip of an

ATM or credit card when that card is inserted through either a specialized card reader or a legitimate payment mechanism (e.g., the card reader used to pay for gas at the pump in a gas station). Once stored, that information can be re-encoded onto any other card with a magnetic strip, instantly transforming a blank card into a machine-readable ATM or credit card identical to that of the victim. In addition, the increased availability of information on the Internet can facilitate identity theft.

For individuals who are victims of identity theft, the costs can be significant and long lasting. Identity thieves can run up debts in the tens of thousands of dollars under their victims' names. Even where the individual consumer is not legally liable for these debts, the consequences to the consumer are often considerable. A consumer's credit history is frequently scarred, and he or she typically must spend numerous hours sometimes over the course of months or even years contesting bills and straightening out credit reporting errors. In the interim, the consumer victim may be denied loans, mortgages, and employment; a bad credit report may even prevent him or her from something as simple as opening up a new bank account at a time when other accounts are tainted, and opening a new account is essential. Moreover, even after the initial fraudulent bills are resolved, new fraudulent charges may continue to appear, requiring ongoing vigilance and effort by the victimized consumer.

Although comprehensive statistics on the prevalence of identity theft are not currently available, the data suggest that the incidence of identity theft has been increasing in recent years.[14]

Financial identity theft is an *outcome* of identity theft rather than a *type* of identity theft. This occurs after your personal information has been compromised. Once a thief has accessed your Social Security Number, name, address, phone number, bank account number, credit card, debit card, PIN, or password, he or she uses this information to open new financial accounts or to take over your existing accounts, with the ultimate goal of getting paid, whether by siphoning

---

[14] "Prepared Statement of the Federal Trade Commission on Financial Identity Theft," Federal Trade Commission, April 22, 1999, http://www.ftc.gov/os/1999/04/identitythefttestimony.htm.

money out of your accounts or by obtaining credit in your name.

#20: What Is New Account Fraud?

New account fraud refers to financial identity theft in which the victim's personal identifying information and credit standing are used to create new accounts, which are then used to obtain products and services. Thieves often use their victim's Social Security Number to commit new account fraud. Since the thief typically uses a different mailing address when applying for new accounts, the victim never receives the bills, and may remain unaware of the account's existence until creditors come seeking payment for debts that have been accumulated in the victim's name without his or her knowledge.

New account fraud includes:

- **Utility fraud:** The identity thief opens new utility accounts (gas, electric, phone, or cable) in the victim's name. This accounts for as much as 20 percent of all instances of identity theft.
- **Loan fraud:** In order to obtain a loan for a car, boat, home, or even a smaller "payday" loan, applicants are almost

always required to provide a Social Security Number. Loan fraud accounts for approximately 10 percent of instances of identity theft.

- **Credit card fraud:** Credit card fraud is the most lucrative type of new account fraud, and the most prevalent—accounting for almost half of all identity theft cases. Identity thieves love credit cards because they are the easiest accounts to open, and they can turn them into cash the fastest.

- **Instant credit:** Instant credit means instant identity theft. Identity thieves salivate when they obtain personal identification information and are in the range of a major retailer offering instant credit.

Easy credit is the foundation of a credit-driven society, and the recession hasn't significantly dampened the issuance of credit cards. Consumers receive millions of pre-approved credit card applications in their mailboxes every year. Credit cards are generally issued to those of legal age, which is over the age of 18, but children as young as 15 years old may be able to piggyback on their parents' credit cards. As soon as they graduate high school or become adults, however, they are treated just like their parents. If there are 200 million people who are 18 years old and over who are receiving applications, that is a lot of junk mail that goes into the trash.

Identity thieves figured out a long time ago that pre-approved credit card applications hold a degree of credibility in the eyes of the issuing bank. After all, the bank mailed the application to the intended recipient, so when the application is returned with most of the applicant's information appearing correct, the bank issues the card. It is not uncommon to learn about pre-approved credit card applications that have been torn up (by hand), and then taped back together, filled out, and mailed in by an identify thief—and a credit card was issued soon after. Why? In the eyes of the bank, all the data checks out, so the application must be legitimate.

Internet and telephone applications are just as easy to scam, due to the anonymity of the transactions. An identity thief only needs a few pieces of key information—name, address, and Social Security Number—and they are off and running. While these applications are often traceable, public computer terminals and disposable cell phones all but ensure a thief's anonymity.

#21: What Is Account Takeover Fraud?

Account takeover fraud refers to financial identity theft in which the victim's account information (a credit card number, for example) is used to charge products and services to his or her existing accounts. Victims often detect account takeover when they discover charges on their monthly statements that they did not authorize, or funds depleted from existing accounts.

The most common types and methods of account takeover fraud are:

- **Credit Card Fraud:** The words "credit card" and "security" go together like "hot" and "ice." In other words, they simply do not go together at all. For the credit card holder, security may consist of entering a personal identification number (PIN) or zip code, verifying a signature, or providing identification. In transactions where you don't have to physically show someone your card, security might consist of a card verification value (CVV) code, which is intended to verify that the user is in control of the card. With the exception of entering a PIN, none of these security features are proactive or in any way constitute adequate security. Even a PIN can be compromised in a number of different ways. It is a little-known fact that a credit card holder has the right to refuse to show additional identification. In fact, asking for a cardholder's identification is usually a violation of the merchant's agreement with credit card companies. Furthermore, when a cardholder elects to sign his or her name, "See Driver's License" or "CID" or "See ID," the holder is, in fact, voiding the agreement with the card issuer, because all terms and agreements are acknowledged via a handwritten signature on the card itself.

- **Hacking:** Cracking unprotected data, or even cracking what's considered protected data under the Payment Card Industry standards, has become the bane of banking, financial, retail, and credit card processing companies. Criminal hackers have found numerous techniques for accessing data that can be turned into cash.
- **Scams:** As criminal hackers get more sophisticated in their online scamming,

they are also becoming more proficient at persuading consumers to hand over their credit card data, using a variety of ruses, both online and in the real world.

- **Skimming:** ATMs, gas pumps, and any debit card or point-of-sale credit card readers are all susceptible to skimming. When you use any of these machines, you swipe your credit or debit card so the machine can read the credit card's magnetic strip. Criminals have perfected the art of manufacturing hardware skimmers that are placed on the face of ATMs or other devices over or near where a card is swiped. These devices record the data off the magnetic strip and retrieve the user's PIN code via tiny cameras placed in view of the keypad. Once the data is stolen, the criminals who planted the skimming device can use the stolen information to create a functional credit card.

- **Phishing:** Anyone who uses email has undoubtedly received an email from a criminal posing as a bank, PayPal, AOL, eBay, or any other entity that might have a reason to access the consumer's bank account, or through third parties where the bank account may be linked. Recipients often freely enter the data requested in the email, providing usernames, passwords, and additional forms of authentication that allow criminals full access to their accounts. Once a recipient clicks on a link within the body of a phishing email, he or she may be redirected to a spoofed website that mimics the identity of a real brand, which will either requesting additional data or infect the visitor's computer with a virus.

- **Telephone fraud:** Scammers have been using the telephone to commit fraud since its invention. Common victims are the elderly or others that may be less aware of these ruses. By posing as an authority figure, a thief may be able to convince a target to provide all the necessary data necessary to obtain full access to the target's accounts.

- **Phexting or smishing:** Today, we use mobile phones to conduct the same electronic financial transactions we can perform on our computers. It is a common tactic for scammers to send phishing messages via text, which is known as phexting or smishing. Users are prompted to respond with sensitive login data. It is best to delete any messages of this nature.

- **Mortgage refinance fraud:** Unfortunately, much of the information necessary to fraudulently refinance a mortgage or obtain a home equity line of credit in someone else's name can be found online, in a filing cabinet accessible to rogue employees, or even in the victim's trash or a public dumpster, if paperwork has been improperly discarded. This is a combination of account takeover and new account fraud that can often be stopped with a consumer security or credit freeze. An important precautionary step is to establish a strong relationship with your lenders and inquire about any services they may have to help detect this kind of account takeover.

#22: What Is Affinity Fraud?

The U.S. Securities and Exchange Commission defines affinity fraud as:

> *Affinity fraud refers to investment scams that prey upon members of identifiable groups, such as religious or ethnic communities, the elderly or professional groups.*

The fraudsters who promote affinity scams frequently are—or pretend to be— members of the group. They often enlist respected community or religious leaders from within the group to spread the word about the scheme, by convincing those people that a fraudulent investment is legitimate and worthwhile. Many times, those leaders become unwitting victims of the fraudster's ruse.

These scams exploit the trust and friendship that exist in groups of people who have something in common. Because of the tight-knit structure of many groups, it can be difficult for regulators or law enforcement officials to detect an affinity scam. Victims often fail to notify authorities or pursue their legal remedies, and instead try to work things out within the group. This is particularly true where the fraudsters have used respected community or religious leaders to convince others to join the investment.

Many affinity scams involve "Ponzi" or pyramid schemes, where new investor money is used to make payments to earlier investors to give the false illusion that the investment is successful. This ploy is used to trick new investors to invest in the scheme and to lull existing investors into believing their investments are safe and secure. In reality, the fraudster almost always steals investor money for personal use. Both types of schemes depend on an unending supply of new investors—when the inevitable occurs, and the supply of investors dries up, the whole scheme collapses and investors discover that most or all of their money is gone.[15]

#23: What Is Criminal Identity Theft?

Perhaps the most insidious form of identity theft is criminal identity theft, which occurs when someone impersonates the identity theft victim while committing a crime or being arrested. The perpetrator is generally prepared with a forged identification that displays the identity theft victim's name and other information alongside the imposter's picture. When the criminal is cited or arrested for any crime (traffic violations, drug offenses, or violent crimes are common examples), he or she will often post bail and then skip

---

[15] "Affinity Fraud: How to Avoid Investment Scams that Target Groups ," U.S. Securities and Exchange Commission, last modified September 6, 2006, http://www.sec.gov/investor/pubs/affinity.htm.

any ensuing court hearings. When the perpetrator defaults, a warrant is issued in the name of the identity theft victim.

Because of the simplicity of our systems of identification, fake IDs and all the necessary documentation to impersonate someone else on paper are often fairly easy to create. Virtually anyone with a home computer, scanner, and printer can create a fake ID or buy one online.

Victims of criminal identity theft are often arrested for the crimes of the identity thief. Victims have been arrested after being pulled over for minor traffic violations, after the victim's name has been run through a police database. Some victims are even arrested at their own homes, after law enforcement issues an arrest warrant and knocks on the victim's door in the middle of a family dinner. Some victims have been arrested multiple times for the crimes of the thieves who stole their identities.

#24: What Is Identity Cloning?

Of all forms of identity theft, identity cloning may be the most unnerving and bizarre. Identity cloning generally encompasses all aspects of identity theft. In these particular cases, though, thieves are actually intentionally living, functioning, and posing as their victims.

People who clone identities do so for numerous reasons. They may be hiding in plain sight because they are running from the law or evading child support, or they could be mentally ill. These identity cloners often register for schools, gain employment, get married, and have children while using the names and identities of their victims.

Perpetrators of this crime often assume the identities of missing children, elderly people, or the recently deceased. They target these populations because they are the least active in the credit-driven society, and the criminal is less likely to be exposed.

The identity cloner generally has inside knowledge of his or her victim, which can be used to procure the victim's Social Security Number and other basic information necessary to clone the victim's identity. Alternatively, the cloner may read about potential victims in news reports or obituaries. Cloners generally do their best to stay under the radar and will generally act responsibly while under their victim's identity, participating in society to avoid attracting attention to their crime. They often open credit accounts and pay the bills on time.

Victims may never know they have been cloned. They may never experience any adverse effects of having been cloned. Or they may find out in a number of ways—as a result of a bill collector contacting them, for example, or when unusual activity appears on credit reports or tax returns, or after being arrested for a crime.

#25: What Is Medical Identity Theft?

Perhaps the deadliest form of identity theft is medical identity theft. Medical identity thieves have a variety of motives. When financial gain is the motivation for stealing medical identifiers and insurance cards, the crime is considered account takeover fraud. True medical identity theft occurs when the thief's motivation is use someone else's identity to obtain medical procedures or healthcare.

Insurance cards, or just the information printed on insurance cards, can generally allow access to a hospital or doctor's office. If the facility requests additional forms of identity, the thief either runs or produces fake IDs. Sometimes the thief is in cahoots with someone at the facility, who might be willing "sweetheart" the transaction, allowing the thief entry even if it is against procedure.

Insurance cards can easily be counterfeited and are often lost or stolen. The mere possession of an insurance card, any insurance card at all, is often a free pass. Hospitals rely on the honor system when admitting patients, believing that the patients are who they say they are and the administrators are doing their jobs ethically.

Victims of medical identity theft can face the harshest penalty of all—death. When a thief uses a stolen identity in order to procure medical care, the information about the thief's medical condition and diagnosis is added to the victim's medical record. This can result in misdiagnosis and the introduction of information that may be contrary to the victim's medical history or medical conditions. Drugs that the victim may be allergic to or other health issues may not be considered. When discovered, getting this information removed from the victim's medical record can be extremely difficult.

#26: What Is Business or Commercial Identity Theft?

Business or commercial identity theft occurs when a thief uses an existing business' name to obtain credit, or bills a business's legitimate clients for products and services. Often, but not always, a Social Security Number of a company officer is required to commit business identity theft. Other identifiers, such as Federal IDs or Employer's Identification Numbers are readily available in public records, dumpsters, or internally, and the relative ease of access to these identifiers facilitates this crime. Perpetrators of business identity theft are often employees or former employees with direct access to financial documentation. They have the opportunity to pad the books in favor of their scheming.

Victims of business identity theft often do not find out about the crime until significant losses accumulate, or someone discovers discrepancies on the books Because of the hidden nature of the transactions, businesses can lose vast amounts of money. Business identity theft can remain undetected for years.

#27: What Is Child Identity Theft?

Child identity theft occurs when the identity of someone under the age of 18 is compromised. When this occurs, the thief uses the child's Social Security Number to open up new accounts. These new accounts could be anything from credit cards to bank loans to automobile loans. The child's information is used on the initial application for credit, but usually the date of birth is altered to make the child appear older. On the application for credit, a 2-year-old may be listed as a 22-year-old. When this happens, it can adversely affect the child's credit standing later in life, once he or she turns 18 and tries to begin establishing a legitimate credit history.

The Federal Trade Commission estimates that there are 500,000 new victims of child identity theft every year. When a total stranger gets his hands on your child's Social Security Number, he can do all kinds of damage. Sometimes, however, the culprits are parents, who have direct access to their children's Social Security Numbers. When irresponsible parents apply for credit in their child's name due to existing financial hardships, the destruction of the child's credit file begins.

You are probably saying, "Of course I would never steal my own child's identity." But sometimes the custodial parent discovers that his or her former spouse or partner committed identity theft when notices from bill collectors begin arriving. Creditors often fail to verify an applicant's age, and simply accept a credit application at face value. Children rarely discover that they are victims of identity theft until they are adults, when they are denied student loans or even jobs.

When identity theft occurs, it ultimately affects a person's ability to function. No matter what type of identity theft, it ends up consuming the victim's day-to-day activities as he or she goes through a long, arduous process of rectifying and restoring his or her identity. The actions of an identity thief can range from opening new accounts to committing a crime, or a thief could even get married and have children using someone else's name. That is a lot of damage to fix!

You spend your life maintaining an upstanding, credible status, yet someone can come along at any point in time and soil your good name. Consumers need to be vigilant in monitoring their personal information and protecting themselves from any type of identity theft.

PART TWO:

ONLINE ATTACKS

CHAPTER 4

COMPUTER HACKING BASICS—VIRUS 101

When we think of a virus, we usually envision an organism that we picked up somewhere, which negatively affected our health because our resistance levels were low. A computer virus is basically the same thing. There are computer viruses that can live dormant within your machine and come to life when stimulated, and others you pick up from downloading something that contains a virus or from visiting an infected website—all because your computer's immune system (or security system) is compromised.

I often receive emails from men and women of all ages whose identities have been stolen. They are almost always unable to tell me how it happened. Upon further investigation, we typically find out that their computers have been hacked, usually because the identity theft victim visited a website to play a game or download music, and this allowed a virus to infiltrate his or her PC or Mac. At this point, the victims had no idea that their hard drives now contained executable software programs that would allow hackers to remotely access their computers from anywhere in the world, and to view all of their files at any time.

Having secured access to a victim's computer, a hacker will often log all of the user's keystrokes, giving the hacker a record of any websites visited, as well as all the usernames and passwords typed on the keyboard. In addition to that, all the files stored on the victim's computers are exposed, potentially including sensitive personal information like names, addresses, and Social Security Numbers of the primary user and of children and family members. This gives the criminal hacker all the information needed to create new accounts under their names.

#28: How Do I Maintain Optimal Health for My Computer?

Just as you maintain your own health on a daily basis by eating well-balanced meals, getting plenty of rest, and exercising, you must also maintain your computer's health. That means avoiding actions that would negatively affect your computer, like visiting dangerous websites or downloading infected programs, videos, or games. It also means making sure the security technology incorporated into your computer, such as antivirus and anti-spyware software, is up to date. You also need to ensure that your wired or wireless Internet connection is secure.

#29: What Can a Virus Do to My Computer?

A virus can do a number of different things to a person's computer. In the late 1990s and early 2000s, the main purpose of computer viruses was to wreak havoc by, for example, deleting files, scrolling profanity across the screen, or crashing a computer by sending it into an endless loop of turning on and turning off.

By the mid-2000s, viruses became much more sophisticated, allowing operators to remotely access infected computers and enabling keystroke loggers and screenshots, through which hackers could monitor any and all user activity. These newer viruses opened the door for hackers to collect all the personal information they needed to compromise victims' existing accounts.

#30: How Does a Virus Get Onto My Computer?

A virus can enter your computer in a number of different ways. If you do not have updated security patches for your operating system, there are probably vulnerabilities that will allow a virus to slip through. If you don't have the latest version of your Internet browser, there may be susceptible areas through which a virus could enter. A vulnerable computer can become infected after a virus injects code via your Internet browser. Or you might open an attachment from someone you know, whose files have already been infected. You might click a link in the body of an email that automatically downloads a virus. You may even be involved in illegal file sharing and inadvertently download an infected file.

These are just a few of the many ways a virus can get onto your computer.

#31: How Does Social Networking Risk My Security?

Social media security issues include identity theft, brand hijacking, compromised privacy, online reputation management, and the user's physical security. One of the easiest ways into a company's network is through social media. Social networking websites have grown too big, too fast, and many websites and website users fail to keep up with the latest security precautions.

Social media provides opportunities for criminals to "friend" their potential victims, creating a false sense of trust they can use against their victims through phishing or other scams. Criminals know exactly how to take advantage of this, so we need policies and procedures that outline appropriate measures, and we need to remember to be vigilant of social networking scams.

#32: What Is a "Drive-By Download?"

A drive-by download refers to the unintentional download of a virus or malware onto a computer.

This can be occur when you intentionally download an apparently legitimate program, or if you click on a link without realizing a virus is attached, or visit a rogue website containing viruses that infect your computer.

#33: What Is Wardriving?

Wardriving refers to the random search for wireless Internet access by driving through neighborhoods, office parks, and any other highly populated areas, looking for an unsecured Internet connection. This becomes dangerous when a wardriver succeeds in locating an open connection that allows access to your computer's hard drive. The potential thief can then search your computer for personal data or use your wireless connection for other nefarious purposes.

#34: Is There Such a Thing As a Good Virus?

When something is labeled a "virus," it means there is a problem of some kind. But computer viruses can be categorized according to different threat levels, which indicate how invasive and potentially damaging a particular virus is. There are viruses that will annoy you, and then there are those that allow thieves to steal your identity.

While one may be less dangerous than another, there is no such thing as a good virus.

If you download a program with a virus attached, the program may be fully functional, but the virus that comes along with it can still be eradicated by antivirus software.

#35: How Do I Know If My Computer Has a Virus?

If your computer is running the latest version of a reputable antivirus program, it should recognize a virus that is already on your computer or even one that's about to be downloaded. It is important that your antivirus software is set to scan your computer at regular intervals and automatically download updates to antivirus definitions. It should be able to recognize a virus attempting to infect your computer or one that is already there. While there are always new viruses that the antivirus program may not yet recognize, it is likely that a future antivirus definition update will soon allow the software to detect and eradicate the latest virus.

A good antivirus program will immediately quarantine any virus it detects. Once the virus has been quarantined, you may be asked what you want to do with it—either immediately delete it, or put it aside. There may be some instances where an antivirus program will consider a file a virus when it is not a virus, but rather a legitimate program or a file that a legitimate program uses regularly. The quarantine feature allows you to restore a file or program you know is safe prior to deletion.

#36: What's The Best Way to Get Rid of a Virus on My Computer?

Your security software, such as McAfee Total Protection™, generally includes instructions for removing or quarantining viruses and malicious programs that infect your computer. If you are functioning in a Windows environment, Microsoft offers tools to remove malware. With antivirus software and the protection provided by your operating system, you have the basic tools needed to defend against most viruses.

There are important steps you can follow to ensure your computer is free:

• Scan for viruses on your desktop computer, laptop or netbook on a regularly scheduled basis—weekly is ideal for deep scans, but you should run a quick scan daily, if possible.

- Your antivirus program's settings should be scheduled to automatically update. If not, you should manually update your antivirus software on a daily basis.

- Set your email program to notify you before downloading pictures or executable files. If possible, set your email to only display text, and to prompt you before loading any pictures or links.

- Never click on a link or download any file that comes from an email address that you do not recognize. If you want to visit a link from an unknown recipient, go to your bookmarks to access the website, browse for the page, or manually type the web address (URL) into your Internet browser's address bar.

Technology doesn't have to be scary or over-whelming. It does, however, require you to increase your security intelligence. Remember, bad guys are systematically applying techniques to hack your data and obtain your information. In response, you must be proactive in keeping your antivirus and security software up to date in order to protect yourself.

CHAPTER 5

HOW CYBER-CRIMINALS STEAL YOUR IDENTITY

Cybercriminals steal your identity by first compromising a database containing your personal information. That database may belong to a major corporation, a government agency, or your doctor's office. Once the hackers find their way into the system, they have access to data that may include Social Security Numbers or credit card information. As discussed in previous chapters, identity thieves either want to take over existing accounts or open up new accounts.

These criminals are constantly hunting for security holes that will allow them to find the path of least resistance into a company's or government agency's network. They exploit vulnerabilities present in old or outdated operating systems or browsers. They can even gain access through wireless Internet connections. In today's climate, cyber attacks are common, and entities responsible for housing and protecting our data are being targeted at an alarmingly high rate.

While security professionals strive to protect our data, hackers are always finding new ways around security measures. In a recent survey, hundreds of companies worldwide estimated that they had lost a combined $4.6 billion in intellectual property as a result of data breaches, and have spent approximately $600 million repairing the damage. Based on these numbers, McAfee projects that companies lost more than one trillion dollars in the last year. There are several motives for this type of theft, but the most common is to steal identities.

I was recently contacted by a woman who said a pop-up window appeared on her desktop, warning that her antivirus program was out of date. She was instructed to update the antivirus program and pay a license fee. In the process of clicking the links in the directions and entering her information, another pop-up window appeared, with a customer service representative requesting remote access to her computer, supposedly in order to complete the upgrade and scan for security vulnerabilities. When the woman granted access to the customer service representative, she was told that she had a virus on her system that required immediate removal, which would cost an additional $156.

During this process, not only did she permit an unknown stranger to access her computer remotely, she also provided the customer service representative with her credit card information. It turned out that the first pop-up window was not actually from her antivirus software provider, nor was the message from the so-called "customer service agent"—it was a cybercriminal pretending to represent her antivirus software company. The charges for the service and the antivirus software were not for any legitimate product; this woman was a victim "scareware."

#37: What Do the Terms "Malware," "Spyware," "Trojan Horse," and "Root-kit" Mean?

- **Malware:** "Malware" is a shortened version of the term "malicious software."

It can apply to any type of invasive software, from a virus to a Trojan horse. Basically, anything that enters your computer without your knowledge or consent and is intended to cause harm or steal data from your computer is considered malware.

- **Spyware:** Spyware has a single task: to spy on your habits and track the information you provide to websites, such as your account information, credit card numbers, and passwords. It then sends all the information it has gathered back to its creator.

- **Trojan horse:** As in tales from Greek mythology, a Trojan horse sneaks onto a computer disguised as something perfectly harmless, or maybe even helpful. It could even be disguised as an antivirus program. However, it is designed to steal information from a computer's hard drive, or to destroy it completely.

- **Root-kit:** Root-kits are the hardest type of invasive software to detect, and they are nearly impossible to remove once they have infiltrated a system. As implied by the name, root-kits dig into the roots of a hard drive. They are designed to steal passwords and identifying information and, even with free antivirus software, the victim often has no knowledge of what is happening.

#38: What Is Phishing?

Fishing, of course, is the sport of tossing a baited hook into the water and then patiently waiting for a fish to bite.

Phishing is similar. The cyber crook sends out spam email and waits for a victim to take the bait. A phisher can send thousands of phishing emails a day, and eventually some people will get hooked.

Despite efforts to educate consumers and employees, a carefully crafted email that appears to have been sent by a fellow employee or trusted entity is still the most effective spear phish. "Whaling"—targeting a CEO or other high-level executive with a phishing email—can be even more successful. As they say, the bigger they are, the harder they fall. To protect yourself, never click on links in emails, even if they appear to come from a bank or another see-mingly trustworthy source. Instead, type the address manually or use your bookmarks menu.

Phishing is a multibillion-dollar business. Unlike the ongoing depletion of the ocean's fisheries, there are still plenty of people out there to phish. Today, many victims in developing nations like India and China have only recently gotten broadband Internet access, and are considered fresh meat by the bad guys.

#39: What Is a Botnet?

The word "botnet" is short for robot network, a group of Internet-connected personal computers that have been infected by a malicious application that allows a hacker to control the infected computers without alerting the computers' owners. Since the infected computers are controlled remotely by a single hacker, they are known as bots, robots, or zombies.

When a virus recruits an infected computer into a botnet, a criminal hacker is able to remotely control that computer and can often access all the data on that computer.

Botnets have a varied history. A "bot" is a program designed to connect to a server and execute a command or series of commands. As reported by a McAfee study, networks of bots, otherwise known as drones or zombies, are most often used to commit cybercrime. This can include "stealing trade secrets, inserting malware into source code files, disrupting access or service, compromising data integrity, and stealing employee identity information. The results to a business can be disastrous and lead to the loss of revenue, regulatory compliance, customer confidence, reputation, and even of the business itself. For government organizations, the concerns are even more far reaching."[16]

In the second quarter of 2010, more than two million computers were recruited into botnets in the United States alone. That's more than five out of every 1,000 personal computers. The rise and proliferation of botnets will continue to put identities at risk.

Computers with old, outdated, or unsupported operating systems like Windows 95, 98, and 2000 are extremely vulnerable. Systems using old or outdated browsers such as Internet

---

[16] Zheng Bu, Pedro Bueno, Rahul Kashyap, and Adam Wosotowsky, "The New Era of Botnets," McAfee Labs, September 2010, http://www.mcafee.com/us/resources/white-papers/wp-new-era-of-botnets.pdf.

Explorer 5 or 6, or older versions of Firefox offer a path of least resistance.

#40: What Is Typosquatting?

Typosquatting, also known as URL hijacking, is a form of cybersquatting that targets Internet users who incorrectly type a website address into their web browser (e.g., "Gooogle.com" instead of "Google.com"). When users make a typographical error while entering the address, they may be led to an alternative website owned by a cybersquatter or criminal hacker.

Typosquatters often create spoofed websites that imitate the look and feel of the intended destination. Operations like these sometimes exist to sell products and services that are in direct competition with those sold at the website you had intended to visit, but they may also be a front to steal personal identifying information, including credit cards or Social Security Numbers.

In some cases, typosquatters employ phishing in order to get you to visit their spoofed websites. For example, when AnnualCreditReport.com was launched, dozens of similar domain names with intentional typos were purchased, which soon played host to fake websites designed to trick visitors. In cases like this, phishing emails sent by scammers spoofing a legitimate website with a typosquatted domain name make for tasty bait. Typosquatting and phishing go hand in hand.

#41: What Is Ransomware?

Data can sometimes be held hostage with the help of "ransomware," also known as "ransom software." This software infiltrates your computer when you download an infected attachment or clicking a link within the body of an email. You can also get ransomware simply by visiting the wrong website, in what is called a "drive-by."

Computerworld reported that a hacker contacted a government agency, threatening to expose health data and demanding $10 million. The alleged ransom note posted on the Virginia DHP Prescription Monitoring Program website claimed that the hacker had backed up and encrypted more than eight million patient records and 35 million prescriptions, and then deleted the original data. The hacker's message read, in part,

"Unfortunately for Virginia, their backups seem to have gone missing, too. Uh oh." [17]

Once your computer is infected with ransomware, it locks down your files to prevent you from accessing them and gives a hacker full control of your machine. Sometimes the ransomware poses as a "Browser Security" or "Anti-Adware" security application whose license has expired. Windows machines that are infected by the ransomware are confronted by a full-screen message that resembles a Windows error alert.

This type of exploitive program is not common, but it's definitely a rising malware threat. The best way to avoid ransomware is to make sure that your computer is running the most current version of your operating system and has updated antivirus software and definitions. It's also very important not to click on links in the body of an email or visit rogue websites that may

---

[17] Jaikurmar Vijayan, "'Hacker' Threatens to Expose Health Data, Demands $10 Million," *ComputerWorld*, May 6, 2009, http://www.computerworld.com/s/article/9132625/_Hacker_threatens_to_expose_health_data_demands_10M?source=rss_null17.

contain viruses that will attempt to inject themselves through any security vulnerabilities in your browser.

#42: What Is Scareware?

Scareware appears on your computer as a pop-up window. It disguises itself as a legitimate warning, but the message is nothing but a ruse intended to scare you into revealing personal identifying information.

Once you have agreed to the scareware's prompt, it begins scanning your computer. It often takes a screenshot of your "My Computer" window and then mimics your computer's characteristics, which will subsequently facilitate tricking you into clicking on links. The scan informs you that a virus has infected your computer, but that for $49.95 you can download software that appears just in time to save the day. From that point forward, if you don't download and install the recommended software, it will feel like pop-up windows have invaded your computer.

Web pages may be infected with or built to distribute scareware. The goal of scareware is to trick you into clicking on links and downloading their software. The rogue software often comes equipped with a customer support link leading to a live session with the bad guy. Real scammers offer live remote access support once a victim has clicked on one of their links. Once you have allowed a scammer to connect remotely, he or she can potentially retrieve documents to steal your identity.

A new twist on scareware involves a pop-up window which mimics an Internet browser and contains a warning indicating that the website has an expired security certificate, a malware warning, or that it might be a phishing website. The window is usually red with a warning: "Visiting This Site May Harm Your Computer." It also provides you with a link, button, or pop-up window that gives you the option of down-loading security software or updating your browser's security.

The software is sometimes called "AntiVirus2010," "WinFixer," "WinAntivirus," "DriveCleaner," "WinAntispyware," "AntivirusXP," "XP Antivirus 2010," or "Security Toolkit." These are actually viruses or spyware that infect your computer, or, at best, junk software that does nothing of value.

What makes scareware so believable is the follow-through, once you have purchased software that is supposed to protect you. There is a shopping cart, an order form, credit card processing, and a download, just like any online software purchase.

#43: What Is a Keylogger?

Spyware sometimes takes the form of a keylogger, which is a type of software, or a key-catcher, a piece of hardware similar to a USB flash drive, which connects to a computer through the USB port and piggybacks on the keyboard connection. Key-catchers are most prevalent in schools, where students plug them into the back of teachers' computers, trying to get test information ahead of time.

In England, two key-catchers were found plugged into public library computers. If the USB devices had not been discovered, they would have allowed whoever planted them to access a record of keyboard activity on the compromised computers. [18]

#44: What Is a RAT?

When a RAT, or "Remote Access Trojan," or "Remote Administration Tool," is coupled with spyware, it can capture every keystroke you type, take a snapshot of your screen, and even record video of your screen. Most dangerously, it obtains full access to all of your files. If you use a password manager, which is software designed to store and enter website passwords, they have access to that program and all your saved login credentials.

RATs covertly monitor a computer without the user's knowledge. A common RAT to be aware of is the "Backdoor Orifice," which is a remote access tool that provides a hacker with system administrator privileges on your computer.

---

[18] John Leyden, "Hardware Keyloggers Found In Manchester Library PCs," *The Register*, February 15, 2011, http://www.theregister.co.uk/2011/02/15/hardware_k eyloggers_manchester_libraries/

RATs can be installed manually by anyone with onsite access to a machine, as well as when a user opens an infected attachment, clicks links in a pop-up window, or installs a helper toolbar or any other software that only appears to be legitimate. RATs have even been installed after the victim picks up a thumb drive found on the street or in a parking lot and plugs it into a computer. Even off-the-shelf computer peripherals like digital picture frames or extra hard drives can be infected before they have left the factory. Cybercriminals can also trick victims into downloading RATs while playing online video games.

#45: What Are Peer-to-Peer (P2P) File-Sharing and the Associated Risks?

Peer-to-peer (P2P) file-sharing is a great technology used to share data over the Internet with others using the same software. It's also a great way to be exposed to hackers and have your identity stolen.

If not properly installed, P2P software allows anyone, including criminal hackers, to access your data. This can result in data breaches, credit card fraud, and identity theft. There are numerous reports of government agencies, drug companies, mortgage brokers, and others discovering P2P software on their networks after personal data has been leaked.

President Obama's helicopter plans, security details, and notes on Congressional depositions have all been leaked on government-controlled computers via P2P. I did a story with a Fox News reporter about a local family with four children, including a 15-year-old with an iPod full of music, but no money. I asked her dad where she got her music, and he replied, "I have no idea." He had no clue that his daughter had installed P2P software on the family computer and was unintentionally sharing all of their data with the world.

There are millions of computers loaded with P2P software, and people are usually clueless that they are exposing their data. P2P software offers a path of least resistance into a user's computer. Be smart and make sure you aren't opening a door to identity thieves.

In summary, despite the silly labels and odd terminology associated with criminal hacking, there is nothing funny about any of these sophisticated techniques used to steal people's identities. Ultimately, all of these programs and hardware can create chaos in your personal life. Your understanding of these different issues and terms will help you realize what you're up against and what your best options are for protecting yourself, your family, and your business.

CHAPTER 6

PROTECTING YOURSELF ONLINE

New scams emerge daily, and one has to be aware of the options for protecting oneself from cybercriminals. I research and write about online security almost every day, and there is never a shortage of topics for me to discuss.

The Internet can be a dangerous neighborhood, with potential attackers around every corner. We, as citizens, have to do something. The president's cybersecurity adviser, Richard Clarke, wrote in 2009 that the Department of Homeland Security (Richard Clarke, 2009) "has neither a plan nor the capability" to protect our nation's cyber infrastructure. He said companies and individuals "almost uniformly believe that they should fund as much corporate cybersecurity as is necessary to maintain profitability and no more."[19]

Many nations de-emphasize individual responsibility, and some citizens expect their governments to take care of them. However, personal security is your own responsibility, and while you may not be responsible for a crime happening to you, you are the one in the best position to prevent it.

#46: What Does Antivirus Software Do?

Each antivirus program is different in how it operates and what it offers, but the basic structure and purpose are the same.

An antivirus program scans your computer's hard drive and any external drives you may have attached to it. The software looks for definitions of viruses that are known to the program. The scan can be performed either manually or automatically, but the automatic setting is preferable.

---

[19] Richard Clarke, "War from Cyberspace," *The National Interest*, December 22, 2009, http://nationalinterest.org/article/war-from-cyberspace-3278.

It is imperative that you set your antivirus software to automatically update daily, so that when new viruses are created and discovered, the software can quickly recognize and remove them.

The 2010 McAfee Threat Report shows that cybercriminal activity is more aggressive than ever:[20]

- The first six months of 2010 were the most active *ever* for total malware production.
- McAfee sees 60,000 new pieces of malware per day.
- Malware is getting smarter—Zeus, a sophisticated malware that is spread via download or phishing attack, switched from text-based emails to emails containing graphics, to avoid being recognized by anti-spam technologies.
- There are approximately six million new botnet infections per month.

---

[20] McAfee, "Q2 Threat Report Reveals Malware at All Time High," press release, August 10, 2010, http://www.mcafee.com/us/about/news/2010/q3/20100810-02.aspx.

- The number of new phishing websites doubled between the first and second halves of 2010.
- 60 percent of top Google search terms returned malicious sites in the first hundred results.

#47: Should I Purchase Antivirus Software or Use a Free Downloadable Version?

Basic security solutions are often available to consumers at no cost. While this makes them attractive, they only offer elementary antivirus protection, relying solely on a database of known virus signatures to keep consumers protected. The disadvantage of this detection method is that users are only protected from viruses that pre-date their last virus definition update.

McAfee recommends that consumers buy cloud-based, real-time protection. Cloud solutions *proactively* search for new cyber threats and protect users from emerging threats. Once suspicious activity has been identified, researchers isolate, investigate, develop, and deploy countermeasures in *real-time*.

In addition to cloud technology, consumers should have an inbound and outbound firewall, anti-phishing protection, and a website safety advisor that identifies risky websites.

Almost all free antivirus software vendors include links within their programs, which are aimed at selling "premium" or "complete" protection to the user, thereby admitting that the level of security offered by their free offerings is inadequate.

#48: How Do I Protect Myself from Malware?

Use safe search web browsing technology like McAfee® SiteAdvisor™. SiteAdvisor warns of potentially malicious websites by displaying easy-to-understand red, yellow, or green circles beside links displayed in search results, indicating the relative riskiness of each website.

Prevent unauthorized software installation by password-protecting the administrator account on your computer.

Only download files from trusted websites, and avoid downloading torrents and software cracks, which are often seeded with spyware.

Never click "Agree," "OK," "No," or "Yes" when you see a pop-up window. Instead, hit the red "X" or shut down your browser by hitting Ctrl-Alt-Delete. For Macs, press Command-Option-Escape on your keyboard, toggle to the offending application, and click Force Quit. Or tap the Apple logo on the top left corner of your screen, select Force Quit, toggle to the offending application, and click the Force Quit button.

Keep your operating system's security patches updated and be sure to install the latest, most secure version of your Internet browser. You should also run McAfee Total Protection, including spyware removal.

#49: How Do I Protect Myself from Viruses?

As stated many times throughout this book, it is important to stay fully up to date with the latest security software (that is, you should never let your subscription lapse and never cancel automatic updates sent from the security vendor). Virus scans should run automatically and should be set to run once a week. However, the frequency can be changed within the user interface to scan every day, which is recommended. A good rule of thumb is to always maintain a healthy skepticism about emails or other messages that you receive online. If something looks strange or sounds too good to be true, it most likely is.

#50: How Do I Protect Myself from Spyware and a Key-Catcher?

Spyware is a form of malicious software, so to protect yourself from spyware, you should follow all instructions listed in "#48: How Do I Protect Myself from Malware?"

To protect yourself from a key-catcher, check your USB and PS/2 ports for any mysterious devices attached to your computer. While antivirus software is specifically designed to detect malicious programs, it may not recognize a key-catcher, because it is an external device that does not run typical keylogger software. Key-catchers are created to imitate a legitimate hardware device that would be plugged into the back of the computer. For this reason, you must physically inspect your computer to find out if a key-catcher has been placed onto your computer.

Some browsers, such as Firefox, offer an on-screen keyboard to try to circumvent key-catchers, and there are different types of other software-based spyware detectors that can also capture screenshots.

To ensure your safety when entering credit card information online, you should use automatic form filler software that is included with password managing programs.

#51: What Is a Firewall?

A firewall is a piece of hardware or software designed to allow or block incoming and outgoing transmissions between your computer and the Internet. It is configured to permit or deny network transmissions based upon a set of rules.

#52: How Do I Configure My Computer's Firewall to Protect My Information?

Most operating systems come with an inbound firewall already installed, which performs basic functions and determines whether to allow or deny various types of programs based on default settings. A more advanced firewall system, such as the one that comes with McAfee Total Protection, alerts you to any potential data threats coming in or going out, and blocks perceived threats until you allow or deny access manually. With McAfee security software installed, you don't need to configure your firewall. McAfee does this automatically.

Once installed, McAfee security software monitors all data ports in your firewall. If any suspicious activity is detected, such as an attempt to breach the firewall or exit via a port on your computer, the software will immediately act to prevent the action.

#53: What Is "Windows Update?"

Windows Update, also known as "Microsoft Update," scans your computer on a regularly scheduled basis for any necessary software or hardware updates.

You can access Windows Update from your control panel. Make sure it is set to download and update critical security patches automatically.

#54: How Does a Service Pack Protect Me?

Technology and cybercrime evolve rapidly. When security breaches impact programs and operating systems, updates quickly become available to plug these breaches. It is important to install necessary updates as they are suggested by your operating system and security software in order to keep your computer safe and secure.

Just as Windows Update patches holes and secures breaches within your operating system, a service pack is a bundle of upgrades and added enhancements that allow your operating system to run faster and more smoothly, as well as strengthening your protection against potential threats.

The main difference between an update and a service pack is that a service pack delivers several updates at once.

Whether you realize it or not, your computer is one of the biggest threats to your personal security. The current president's administration believes that your computer is also one of the biggest threats to national security.

The message is this: Think before you click. Stop, think, and then connect. Know who's on the other side of that email, torrent, or instant message. Everything you say or do in cyberspace remains in cyberspace, for anyone to find, steal, and use against you or your government.

CHAPTER 7

PROTECTING YOURSELF ONLINE— TAKING IT A STEP FURTHER

Now that you know the basics of online protection, it is time to review additional tools and scam prevention techniques, and to introduce you to new terms and more options to help ensure that you have a safe online experience.

#55: Which Web Browser Is the Safest?

The major web browsers are:

- Microsoft Internet Explorer
- Mozilla Firefox

- Google Chrome
- Safari

While Internet Explorer has taken a beating over the years, it has redeemed itself and become much more secure than it has been in the past. There has been a great deal of debate over which browser is better, faster, and more reliable, but they are arguably almost equal in terms of speed, reliability, and security.

Internet Explorer updates its security protocol whenever a Windows user runs Windows Update. Firefox offers safety features such as automatically scanning all downloaded pictures and programs for viruses and malware, as well as its virtual keyboard. Chrome is considered more website-friendly, as it tends to do better than Firefox when it comes to displaying websites.

Each browser has security features and other options that require the user's attention, as they may or may not be enabled by default:

- Pop-up blockers should be enabled.
- Users must determine whether a browser should remember passwords for various websites, as well as enabling a master

password. For numerous reasons, I'm not a fan of storing passwords.

- Users must select whether content should be downloaded manually or automatically, as well as where the data is stored. In most cases, automatically downloading is not advised.

Typically, users have the option to set their browser to update automatically I, however, prefer to be notified so I can make a determination as to what changes in functionality there may be, or if any plug-ins may not be compatible with the update.

#56: Should I Use a Wired or Wireless Internet Connection?

A simple way to illustrate the security difference between wired and wireless Internet connections is to compare an Internet connection to a telephone cord. When a phone is connected to an outlet with a cord, the line is considered more secure. On the other hand, cordless, handheld, and wireless telephone conversations can be easily intercepted, or "sniffed," by various scanning tools. Of course, a wired connection can be tapped as well, but that requires internal access.

It is similar with wired and wireless Internet connections: when your computer is connected directly to a modem with a wire or cable, the transmission signal cannot be sniffed. However, when a connection is wireless and therefore less secure, the wireless signal can be hacked, and the data and information being transferred can be stolen.

#57: How Do I Protect Myself from Phishing?

To protect yourself from phishing, you must never click on a link in any email from a sender who you do not recognize. If you think it the email is legitimate, hold your cursor over the link to reveal the exact address of the URL. If the address is the correct one for the website you wish to visit, the link should be safe. But it may be slightly different, such as in instances of typosquatting. If you're not sure, call the company or individual who supposedly sent the email, or type the website address directly into your browser's address bar.

If you receive an email alert from a website with an internal messaging system, log in normally and check for new messages, rather than clicking through from the email. If you receive an email notifying you that an online statement is ready, again, go to the website directly, either by using your bookmarks toolbar or typing the address manually, rather than clicking through from an email.

If an email ends up in the spam folder, this may be an indication that it is a phishing email, even if it appears legitimate. Many browsers and email programs now include some form of detection for phishing emails or spoofed websites.

Remember that a legitimate company will never send an email asking you to change your password or email credit card information. If you get any emails along these lines, delete them immediately and notify the company or the FTC. McAfee SiteAdvisor's anti-phishing technology identifies risky websites using color-coded ratings in your search results, to warn you before you go to a risky site. This is a must, to fish out the phishers.

#58: How Do I Prevent My Computer from Becoming a Zombie?

Consumers' and small businesses' relaxed security practices give scammers a base from which to launch attacks, by allowing them to create botnets without being detected. Hackers use botnets to send spam and phishing emails and to deliver viruses and other malware.

A botnet can consist of as few as ten computers, or tens or hundreds of thousands. Millions of personal computers are potentially part of botnets. Computers that aren't properly secured are at risk of being turned into bots, or zombies.

Certain user behaviors can also invite attacks:

- Surfing pornographic websites
- Frequenting gaming websites hosted in foreign countries
- Downloading pirated content from P2P websites

Remember, there is no honor among thieves. Simply put: don't engage in risky online activities that invite attacks.

Computers with old, outdated, or unsupported operating systems like Windows 95, 98, and 2000 are extremely vulnerable. Using old or outdated browsers such as Internet Explorer 5, 6, or older versions of Firefox 3.6 or older makes it easier for cybercriminals to hack your computer.

To protect your PC, keep your critical security patches up to date by setting Windows Update to automatically install the latest service pack, or upgrade to Windows 7. Make sure to set your antivirus software to update automatically as well.

Apple's Mac OS generally responds quickly to online threats and automatically delivers security updates. Mac users have not been vulnerable to the same viruses and threats that have traditionally plagued PCs, but the Internet has leveled the playing field. Mac users are now just as susceptible to online risks as PC users. With increasingly popularity of Apple's operating system, hackers and thieves are focusing their efforts to develop attacks that will work on Macs.

Apple's Security Update page instructs, "Be sure that you are running the latest version of system software. Apple will release security updates from time to time, and having the latest available system software version should improve the security of your system." For more information check the Apple Security Updates page at support.apple.com/kb/HT1222.

McAfee® Internet Security for Mac offers comprehensive protection against hackers, identity theft, phishing scams, malware, viruses and more. It protects you from dangerous websites, allowing you explore to the web without worry.

#59: How Do I Protect Myself from Typosquatting?

Recently, typosquatters created a website imitating Twitter.com called Tvvitter—that's T-v-v-i-t-t-e-r (cute, huh?). They sent phishing emails to millions of users, many of whom clicked on the link included within the email, which sent them to the phishing site where they attempted to log in by entering their user names and passwords.

To avoid these types of scams:

- When searching online, look carefully before clicking on any link.
- When typing a web address in a browser, check the address bar to confirm you spelled it properly before hitting Enter.
- Do business with online retailers you are familiar with, and take care to type their web addresses correctly, or use book-marks to access their websites.

Use your favorites menu to access frequently visited sites.

#60: How Do I Protect Myself from Ransomware and Scareware?

The best way to avoid being locked out of your own files by a ransomware infection is to make sure that your computer is updated with the most current version of your operating system and the latest antivirus definitions. You can also prevent ransomware from infiltrating your computer by remembering not to click on links within the body of an email and refraining from visiting risky websites that may contain viruses.

To protect your computer from scareware, follow these steps:

- Use the most up to date browser. Whether it's Internet Explorer, Chrome, or Firefox, make sure you have the latest version. At minimum, download any available security updates for your existing browser.
- Use your browser's pop-up blocker. This is usually turned on by default. No pop-ups, no scareware.

- There are some legitimate pop-ups, but if a pop-up window won't let you close it, press Ctrl-Alt-Delete to shut down the browser. For Macs, press Command-Option-Escape on your keyboard, toggle to the offending application, and press Force Quit. Or, tap the Apple logo on the top left corner of your screen, select Force Quit, toggle to the offending application, and press the Force Quit button.

- Never click on links in pop-ups. If the pop-ups are out of your control, do a hard shut down before you start clicking on links.

- Patience and persistence counts. Closing a pop-up window can sometimes be difficult, but any buttons you press within the pop-up could mean downloading the exact virus you're trying to avoid.

- Ensure that your antivirus software is up to date, and keep it set update virus definitions automatically.

Never click on links on a web page that suggests downloading updates for your browser or downloading security software. If possible, click on the X in the upper right corner of the window. If there is no X, shut down your entire browser, or open Windows Task Manager and disable the application.

#61: How Do I Avoid a Drive-By Download?

The best advice I can share about avoiding drive-by downloads is to avoid visiting websites that could be considered dangerous or malicious. This includes pornographic websites, file-sharing websites, websites that are loaded with pop-up windows, and websites that prompt you to download a plug-in before pages will display properly. You should also keep your antivirus software, Internet browser, and operating system up to date.

#62: How Do I Protect Myself from Wardriving?

Wireless networks broadcast messages using radio frequencies and are thus more susceptible to eavesdropping than wired networks.

When setting up a wireless router, there are two different security protocols you can use. Wi-Fi Protected Access (WPA) is a certification program that was created in response to several serious weaknesses researchers had found in the previous standard, Wired Equivalent Privacy

(WEP). WEP was introduced in 1997 and is the original form of wireless network security.

It is best to follow your router's installation wizard or utilize a web-based application to help set up your network securely.

#63: How Do I Protect Myself from P2P File-Sharing Risks?

Here are some tips to protect you from accidentally sharing data on a P2P network:

- The smartest way to stay safe is not to install P2P software on your computer in the first place.
- If you think a family member may have installed P2P software, check for new and unfamiliar applications by reviewing the All Programs Menu. If you see a name you don't recognize, do an online search to find out if it is a P2P application.
- Set administrative privileges to a single user—you—on your computer, to prevent the installation of new software without your knowledge.

- Use comprehensive security software such as McAfee Total Protection, and keep it up to date.
- Make sure your firewall is enabled, and if an application asks you to change your settings to enable access to the Internet, don't allow it.

P2P file-sharing can be tempting, but in most cases, the dangers just aren't worth it.

PART THREE:

OFFLINE ATTACKS

CHAPTER 8

REAL-WORLD ATTACKS

DEFCON, an annual convention that takes place in Las Vegas, has been bringing together all types of hackers since the early 1990s. At a recent DEFCON, a small group set up a fake ATM in front of the convention center's security office, successfully fooling the other hackers in attendance.

I decided that I needed to see for myself how difficult it would be to purchase an ATM and set it up in an unassuming location.

I began my search on eBay, where I found plenty of new and used ATMs ranging from $500 to $2,500. I quickly determined that I did not want to pay this much, not to mention additional shipping charges of around $300. Next, I tried Craigslist, where I found a post about a bar north of Boston that was getting rid of old pool tables, neon Budweiser® signs, and an ATM.

I took a colleague of mine—a white hat hacker—with me to meet a man named Bob at this run-down bar. It was an old dive that was closing down and liquidating its assets. Bob, who rented a room upstairs, was listing and selling the items for the owner. The ATM was stationed next to the bar, coated with the aftermath of five years of spilled beer. I was grateful that they had covered the ATM's keypad with clear plastic.

After my hacker friend referenced the ATM's manual and got it working, he determined that it was worth the financial risk, so we paid $750 (down from the original asking price of $1,000), loaded it onto my trailer, and brought it home to my garage. There is something about having an ATM in your garage that made for a restless night of sleep—like the night before Christmas when I was as a kid. The next day at 5 a.m., I pulled on a pair of rubber gloves, used an entire bottle of Windex and a few rolls of paper towels, and took the ATM apart.

My friend, the hacker, arrived at my garage with the manual in hand. Giddy with anticipation, he said, "Watch this," and then punched in the master codes to access the machine's data on a memory chip called an "EPROM." A printout of hundreds of credit and debit card numbers spewed from the machine and collected in a pile on the floor.

#64: What Is Social Engineering?

Social engineering is the act of manipulating people into performing certain actions or divulging confidential information. The term typically applies to trickery or deception for the purpose of information gathering, committing fraud, or computer system access. In most cases, the attacker never comes face-to-face with the victim. Call them what you want—con artists, grifters, scammers, or thieves—they are simply one thing: liars. Lying is what they do best. They do it casually, and with such conviction that we have no reason not to believe them. Their crafty remorselessness allows them to get away with social engineering, also known as "pre-texting."

#65: How Does Social Engineering Affect People Online and In the Real World?

Social engineering breaks down our ability to trust each other. Social engineering is lies and fraud.

Lying is a learned behavior. One day, as young children, we stumble upon a situation—one that we created or were a party to—and are confronted by someone in authority, most likely a parent or teacher. They ask a question, and rather than answering honestly, we respond with what we think they want to hear. They believe us, and we are relieved of the burden of truth's consequences.

We use this tool of sorts throughout our lives, whenever we feel it will outweigh the benefits of honesty. (Think you don't lie? What is your answer when a cop pulls you over and asks, "Sir, did you know you were speeding?") We lie to others, we lie to ourselves; we all lie, to some degree. It's a survival mechanism. Some people, however, are professional liars, who go far beyond what might be considered a reasonable lie. They use deception to take what belongs to others. These thieves lack empathy for others' feelings. They are greedy. They aren't concerned about the consequences of their actions and the potential harm they may do.

Experienced liars are often so good that they end up in a position of authority and trust. They may be heads of state, CEOs of corporations, judges, or even members of the clergy. For the past year, I've been corresponding with a minister who received an 18-month sentence for identity theft.

What compounds the problem is the naïveté of civilized human beings. Ideally, we are raised to love and respect one another, to be kind and cordial. We are taught to behave and tell the truth, and we expect others to act in kind. Trust is the foundation of functioning in a civilized society. Without some degree of trust, we'd cease to move in a forward direction, constantly living in fear of the dire consequences of venturing outside. If we didn't inherently trust, how could we possibly get behind the wheel of a car and drive down a two-way street with nothing but a yellow, painted line separating us from a head-on collision and imminent death?

When someone lies to us, we usually suspect that something isn't right. Face-to-face contact with another person gives us the opportunity to spot numerous telltale signals that help us discern whether what we're hearing is a truth or a lie. Human communication relies not just on words, but also on body language and tone of voice. We all exude energy toward others, both positive and negative. Negative energy, coupled with certain words, phrases, or gestures, can send a ping to our bellies or prompt the hair on the back of our necks to rise, signaling a primordial instinct to be wary of what we're being told.

Technology has made it easier than ever for thieves to perfect the art of lying. We see thousands of scams and ruses pulled off every day. The key is to understand the lures, motivations, and tactics of the con artist. When you can sense a snake-oil salesman from a mile away, you are much safer and more secure than those who assume they're immune from falling victim to a con artist's lies. Trust is a fundamental and necessary part of life, but balancing trust with a degree of cynicism can go a long way.

DEFCON attendees participated in a competition in which they successfully manipulated employees from certain Fortune 500 companies into providing full details of their companies' inner workings on network computers and software that could easily be used to launch cyber attacks. Some revealed what operating systems they used, as well as their antivirus software, browsers, email addresses, laptop models, virtual private network software information, and even which garbage collectors hauled the companies' trash!

In some cases, the DEFCON tricksters were able to get targets to visit certain websites while on the phone. Remember that the simple act of visiting a website can allow a malicious program to infiltrate your computer if it's not properly protected. Based on answers freely provided to them, social engineers can guide targets to websites that infect the victims' computers.

It's important to recognize that while you are unlikely to be swindled by a person who calls you, it is always possibility. This means your business should always have systems and communication protocols in place, regulating what can be said to whom, when, and why. Training on social engineering and how to prevent it is a must for any company, and is useful for any individual who doesn't want to fall victim to a con artist.

#66: What Is Automated Teller Machine (ATM) Skimming?

ATM skimming occurs when criminals affix or piggyback a device over an ATM's card slot, which resembles the original card slot itself and blends into the face of the ATM. To the untrained eye, there is nothing unusual about the ATM's appearance. Once an ATM user slides his card through the card slot, the information on the magnetic strip is read, or "skimmed." ATM skimming is fairly common because the technology is easy to acquire, and we have not yet adopted new security technology to protect an antiquated, plastic card system.

There are two components that enable criminals to "skim" your data and turn your card number into cash. The first is the skimmer device itself, and the second is a small, wireless camera that reveals the PIN as it is typed into the keypad.

There are a few specific places where these cameras are often disguised:

- Inside a brochure holder on the side of the ATM
- In a light bar above the keypad

- In a cardboard box behind a small mirror
- In a car stereo speaker attached to the face of the ATM

The technology used in ATM skimming has become increasingly sophisticated. Skimmers can incorporate Bluetooth and texting technology that instantly sends data to the criminal. Furthermore, keypads can be compromised by devices that overlay the existing pad and transfer the data wirelessly. Your safest bet, if you must use an ATM, is to use one that is located inside a bank lobby, but it is advisable that you inspect the ATM before swiping your card.

#67: What Is Caller ID Spoofing?

Spoofing is masquerading and falsifying data. Criminals use this technique to hide the phone number of the line they are using and to display a different phone number on the recipient's caller ID. It is similar to email spoofing, in which a message can appear to have been sent from a different email address, or to website spoofing, in which a phishing email links to a fake website. Most people trust their caller IDs, and are unaware of how easily this flawed system can be spoofed and used to commit fraud.

Your imagination could run wild thinking about all the criminal activities that can be accomplished with the help of caller ID spoofing, but this technology can also be helpful in business or when investigating a crime. For instance, caller ID spoofing technology is often sold as a tool for law enforcement officials to disguise themselves when trying to nab suspects. Or, if someone is trying to evade child support, caller ID spoofing may be a legitimate tool to catch the deadbeat parent. It may also be used to investigate a spouse suspected of cheating. In business, doctors who don't wish to reveal their real phone numbers while on call may create spoofed numbers for clients whose phones won't allow blocked numbers to go through.

Unfortunately, caller ID spoofing is most frequently used for fraud. Law enforcement or businesses might have a legitimate use for it, but the same technology makes it easy for criminals to pose as law enforcement authorities, businesses, charities, government agencies, credit card companies, or any other entity that an unsuspecting victim might be inclined to trust.

#68: What Is Mailbox Raiding?

While criminal hackers are cracking databases and stealing millions of electronic records every year, street-level identity thieves are perpetrating a low-tech version of identity theft. Thieves of this nature live in your neighborhood, or near your neighborhood, and engage in mailbox raiding—they steal unopened mail from your mailbox in hopes of obtaining useful information that could provide opportunities for identity theft.

#69: What Can an Identity Thief Gain from Stealing My Mail?

There are several regularly-delivered pieces of mail that are useful for identity theft:

- Bank statements
- Credit cards
- Financial statements
- Utility bills
- Mobile phone bills
- Membership statements
- Checks
- Disbursements of funds
- Credit card offers

- Social Security checks and statements
- Benefit statements
- Employment papers
- Tax information
- Income statements

These sensitive documents contain enough information for an identity thief to take over your existing accounts or open new accounts in your name. While some data is intentionally omitted from paper statements for the sake of privacy, in many cases they still contain enough sensitive details for a thief to impersonate you over the phone in order to obtain even more details— enough to fill in the puzzle pieces of your identity.

#70: What Can an Identity Thief Gain from Dumpster Diving?

When you think of dumpster diving, you probably think of a homeless person in search of his next meal or some other useful item that can be reused or recycled. But the hungry and homeless aren't the only ones who dive into dumpsters; criminals are becoming increasingly aware of the valuable loot they can find in the trash.

Think about the mail you receive on a typical day. What do you do with the credit card offers and old bank statements? Do you shred them? Do you put them in a trash bag and take them out to the curb? What do you think your bank does with transaction forms from your bank transfers or cashed checks? Do you think they shred them or dispose of them safely? The information an identity thief can gain from your mailbox can also be found in the dumpster behind your bank, mortgage broker's office, utility company, or doctor's office, and even in your own garbage.

A colleague of mine recently spent three minutes in a dumpster behind a large bank to see what he could find. In that short period of time, he found records of wire transfers with names, account numbers, and Social Security Numbers of the sender and the recipient. He also found photocopies of checks with Social Security Numbers and business EIN numbers handwritten in the corner. This "dumpster dive" yielded enough information to access bank customers' accounts or to steal their identities. Fortunately, this was just for research and my colleague shredded the documents he found, but this is an example of how much information a thief can gain from dumpster diving.

#71: What Is Vishing?

Vishing is a form of social engineering in which criminals call victims on the phone and attempt to lure them into divulging personal information that can then be used to commit identity theft. The term comes from "voice," and "phishing," which is, of course, the use of spoofed emails designed to trick targets into clicking malicious links. Instead of a simple email, vishing generally relies on automated phone calls, which instruct targets to provide account numbers.

The scammers pose as a specific entity and use a dual approach, contacting their targets through both email and the telephone to reinforce the pretence that the entity being spoofed is repeatedly requesting targets' data. This multi-pronged method is a persistent and, ultimately, convincing method of attack. The best line of defense is to determine whether the communications are legitimate by reaching out directly to the bank, government agency, business, or other entity that is supposedly contacting you.

Techniques that criminals use when vishing include:

- **Wardialing:** This occurs when the visher uses an automated system to call specific area codes with a message involving local or regional banks or credit unions. Once someone answers the phone, a generic or targeted recording plays, requesting that the listener enter bank account, credit, or debit card numbers, along with PIN codes.

- **VoIP:** Voice over Internet Protocol, or VoIP, is an Internet-based phone system that can facilitate vishing by allowing multiple technologies, such as wardialing and caller ID spoofing, to work in tandem. Vishers are known to use VoIP to make calls, as well as to exploit databases connected to VoIP systems.

- **Caller ID spoofing:** This is the practice of causing the telephone network to display a false number on the recipient's caller ID. A number of companies provide tools that facilitate caller ID spoofing. VoIP has known flaws that allow for caller ID spoofing. These tools are typically used to populate the caller ID with a specific bank or credit union, or simply the words "Bank" or "Credit Union."

- **Social engineering:** Social engineering is a fancier, more technical form of lying. Social engineering (or social penetration) techniques are used to bypass sophisticated security hardware and software. The automated recordings used by vishers tend to be relatively professional and convincing.

#72: If I Take the Necessary Steps to Protect Myself in the Real World, Will I Then Be Safe Online?

Criminals are now using a multi-pronged approach to snare their victims. They may pick through your trash, call you on the phone, steal your mail, and employ a number of other real world attacks to get to you. If they need even additional information, though, they will also try to infect your computer.

The sad truth is that most of us will, at some point, get viruses on our computers. Cybercriminals constantly adapt to our evolving electronic means of information exchange, taking advantage of any possible weakness. Viruses are almost inevitable. You can never let your guard down.

Most people consider identity theft to be an issue that only occurs when a criminal hacker compromises personal information and takes over checking accounts or opens up new accounts under your name. The reality is that identity theft most often occurs when thieves gain access to your identifying information via paper records and even the telephone. It is through these more traditional methods that criminals can obtain your name, address, and Social Security Number and then open up new accounts or take over existing accounts.

In summary, with most of these real-world crimes, identity theft protection software won't directly protect you, but can help minimize your risk. The cornerstones of identity theft protection are education and awareness. While you're not responsible for being victimized, you are ultimately in the best position to prevent an attack.

CHAPTER 9

PROTECTING YOURSELF FROM REAL-WORLD ATTACKS

About 25 years ago, I was in a situation where I needed some help. A man appeared out of nowhere and, sensing my desperation, offered me assistance. I accepted. Up until that day, I was "all about me." When I asked this stranger why he had stopped and gone out of his way for me, he answered, "Sometimes people just need help." His simple act of kindness, and those five words, changed my life.

Through this book and my blog posts, I spend a lot of time talking about "bad guys." I point out their motivations, methods, and techniques, and what you—the honest, responsible, civilized person—needs to do to protect yourself and your family.

Writing about personal security issues for a living requires that I read about negative, awful occurrences on a daily basis. But I'm okay with that, because I care about you, and I want to help. Caring lights a fire within me and motivates me to keep you informed. Like a musician is compelled to play, I am compelled to remind you to stay vigilant.

The chances that your identity will be compromised to the extent of most of the examples described in this book are slim, but there is a chance. We are all in this together. We are a community, and we need to be willing to help each other in order to progress. Life goes by quickly.

Throughout each of our lives, we make choices and decisions that determine our destiny. I believe we are in control of about 90 percent of that destiny, with the remaining 10 percent beyond our control. It's generally not what happens to you, but how you choose to respond to, or "deal with," each unforeseen circumstance that determines the outcome.

My goal is to keep you informed of your security options to help you prevent the bad guys from messing up your life. Your goal should be to learn about the threats and put systems in place to minimize your risk, so you aren't the bad guys' next victim.

#73: How Do I Protect Myself from Social Engineering?

It is important you recognize that, while most people who call or email you are generally not attempting to swindle you, there is a possibility that they are. This means that you need to understand that not every email is safe; not every caller is who he says he is; not every person knocking on your door is harmless; and not everyone who walks into your place of business has honest intentions.

Social engineering is a human-on-human con. Technology can help protect you from social engineering on the Internet, so pay attention to warnings and alerts from your security software.

#74: How Do I Protect Myself from ATM Skimming?

You can protect yourself from ATM skimming in the following ways:

- Pay attention to your bank and credit card statements.
- Refute unauthorized transactions within sixty days.
- Use credit cards instead of debit cards, since credit cards provide more protection against fraudulent charges than debit cards, and a compromised credit card is clearly preferable to a drained bank account.
- Pay close attention to details when you use an ATM, and look for anything that seems out of place. If your card gets stuck in the machine, or if you notice anything odd about its appearance, such as wires, double-sided tape, error messages, a missing security camera, or if the ATM seems unusually old and run down, don't use it.
- Search for and use ATMs in more secure locations so you aren't just using any

ATM. Remember, however, that even an ATM at a bank branch is vulnerable.

- Use your free hand to cover your fingers as you enter your PIN on the keypad.

#75: How Do I Protect Myself from Caller ID Spoofing?

Never assume the number displayed on your caller ID is accurate and never share personal information over the phone, no matter what the caller ID says. If a caller tells you that you've won something, or that you stand to lose something, say that you'll be happy to talk but will need a phone number so you can call back. If they refuse, or if you are still suspicious, locate a legitimate number and call to confirm the details.

#76: How Do I Protect Myself from Mailbox Raiding?

You can protect yourself from mailbox raiding by taking the following actions:

- Discontinue paper statements. Electronic statements in your email inbox are more manageable and secure than paper statements, not to mention eco-friendly.

- Get a locking mailbox. You don't have to provide your mail carrier with the key if you purchase the type of mailbox that allows the carrier to insert letters through a small opening but requires a key to remove them.
- Get a post office box and use it for sensitive mail. Post office boxes require a key to obtain the mail inside, and the only other person with access is the postal carrier.
- Call the post office if you go more than a few days without receiving new mail, as it may have been stolen.
- Pay attention to the delivery dates of your bills and bank statements so you will know if they fail to arrive on schedule.
- Request that your information be removed from the lists maintained by the Direct Marketing Association. Eliminate all other unnecessary solicitation to minimize mail that creates a risk.
- Opt out of pre-approved credit card offers by going to Wi-Fi Protected Access.

#77: How Do I Protect Myself from Dumpster Diving?

Don't simply throw away anything containing personal information. When deciding what to discard and what to shred, consider the following:

- Does it include my full name?
- Does it include my address?
- Does it include my Social Security Number?
- Does it include my birth date?
- Does it include my account number?
- Does it include a password?
- Is it a financial statement?
- Does it include any of the above identifying information for any of my family members?

If the answer to any of these questions is yes, shred the document with a crosscut shredder before discarding it. Crumpling up a piece of paper or cutting a credit card in half will not protect your information from cunning thieves.

Keep your crosscut shredder in the area where you keep your mail so it is convenient, and shredding becomes a habit. Immediately shred anything containing identifying information that you intend to discard.

You must remember that while you may be cautious, responsibly shredding documents that include personal identifying information, your bank, mortgage broker, or accountant may not. That's where identity theft protection comes in.

#78: How Do I Protect Myself from Vishing?

Knowledge is the key to defending yourself from vishing. The better you understand how vishing works, the better off you'll be. Read up on vishing incidents. Ask your bank if they provide information about vishing online or in the mail. This type of crime is rapidly evolving and becoming more sophisticated, so it is imperative that you stay up to date.

To protect yourself from vishing, take the following precautions:

- If you receive a phone call from a person or recorded voice requesting personal information, hang up. If you think the call may have come from a business, institution, or organization that you trust, call back directly to confirm the request.

- Don't trust caller ID, which is easily tampered with and offers a false sense of security.

- Call your bank to report any suspected fraud attempts immediately. The sooner you do, the more quickly the scam will be investigated and squashed.

- Document calls in which you disclose any personal information. Note what information was requested, what you disclosed, and, if possible, the phone number or area code of the caller. If you suspect fraud, report all the details to your bank.

#79: How Do I Make Sure My Information Is Safe When Shopping and Banking Online?

- Be suspicious of any offers you receive via email, especially if they sound too good to be true. The same goes for offers via tweets and social media.

- Don't click on links in emails—always go to the source. Use your favorites menu, a bookmark, or manually type the address into your browser.

- Beware of cybersquatting and typosquatting. Pay close attention to the spelling of web addresses or to websites that look trustworthy, but which may be close imitations of the online retailer you are looking for.

- Use secure sites when possible. If you see "https" in the address bar, it's a secure page.

- Beware of eBay scammers. Don't respond to eBay email offers. Review the history of eBay sellers; established sellers should have great feedback.

- Pay attention to your bank and credit card statements. Check them online every two weeks and refute unauthorized charges within two billing cycles.

- Don't use a debit card online. If your debit card is compromised, money can immediately be withdrawn from your bank account. Credit cards have more protection and less liability.

- Avoid paying by check online or through the mail.

- Only do business with people and companies that you know, like, and trust. It's best to buy high-ticket items from retailers that also have a brick-and-mortar location.

Secure your computer. Update your critical operating system security patches, antivirus software, and virus definitions. Never use a public Internet connection when shopping online; always use a secured Internet connection.

#80: What Is the Difference Between HTTP and HTTPS?

Hypertext Transfer Protocol Secure (HTTPS) is a combination of the Hypertext Transfer Protocol with the added security of Transport Layer Security (TLS) and its predecessor, Secure Sockets Layer (SSL).

In simple English, HTTP means that you are connected to the Internet, and HTTPS means that your connection is secure. Until recently, the only websites that used HTTPS to ensure your security were websites that handle monetary transactions or ask for credit card information, such as banks and online retailers.

Some social networking websites have recently integrated HTTPS to allow a more secure connection, but it is not automatic. Look for the option to use HTTPS, and never provide any financial information without first checking the URL for that "S," for security.

#81: Are Public Hotspots and Free Wi-Fi Connections Safe To Use?

Wi-Fi is everywhere. If you travel for business or simply want Internet access while out and about, your options are plentiful. You can sign on at airports, hotels, coffee shops, fast food restaurants, and even airplanes.

There are several security risks associated with accessing the Internet through a wireless connection. Wi-Fi's primary purpose is not security. It was developed for convenience. Wireless networks broadcast messages using radio frequencies and are inherently more susceptible to eavesdropping than wired networks.

Anyone who uses an open, unsecured network risks exposing their data. There are many ways to see who's connected on a wireless connection and to gain access to their information. As more sensitive data is transmitted wirelessly, the need for security increases. Criminal hackers are more sophisticated today than ever before, putting wireless communications at an even higher risk for security breaches.

As a general rule, if you're on someone else's network—secured or unsecured—your data is at risk. There are many ways to see who's using a wireless connection and gain access to their data.

To protect yourself while using a wireless connection:

- Be smart about what kind of data you transmit on a public wireless connection. There is no need to make critical transactions while sipping that macchiato.
- Don't store critical data on a device used outside the secure network. I have a laptop and an iPhone. If they are hacked, there's nothing on either device that would compromise my identity.
- Turn off the Wi-Fi and Bluetooth on your laptop or cell phone when you're not using them. An unattended device emitting wireless signals is very appealing to a criminal hacker.
- Be cautious when using public Wi-Fi connections. You should never do any shopping, banking, or other transactions

that involve sensitive information on a free wireless connection.

Keep your antivirus software and operating system up to date. Make sure your antivirus software is set to update automatically, and that you have installed all of your operating system's critical security patches.

CHAPTER 10

PREVENTING IDENTITY THEFT

Identity theft protection is an important aspect of personal security. Just as you take measures to protect your life, your family, your home, and your personal property, you must also take measures to ensure that the only person using your identity is you.

As a security professional and an expert in the area of identity theft, I'm still confused by some of the many tools and services claiming to help protect individuals from identity theft. There is a fundamental lack of transparency in the protection being advertised. Identity protection, first and foremost, needs to be transparent. You should know what you are getting, what it does, and why or how it will benefit you.

Most identity theft protection services offer some form of insurance or money-based guarantee, along with recovery and restoration assistance, and "monitoring." They rarely provide details regarding what they monitor, how they monitor, or the benefits of their monitoring service. Monitoring can mean anything from searching the web with readily available free search engines, or it can mean searching for your data on a specific set of websites. Monitoring can also refer to credit monitoring, in which the identity theft protection service has a partnership with one or more credit bureaus and alerts you if there is activity on your credit report.

These same services may claim to help victims recover from identity theft, but in the fine print they explain that identity theft recovery is limited to what they have promised to protect, and only *if* their service fails.

An identity theft protection service should inform you when your personal identifying information, such as your name, Social Security Number, or credit or debit card number, are used to commit fraud or other crimes.

Identity theft protection must keep pace with the evolving criminal landscape and offer multiple layers of proactive monitoring, detection, automatic alerts, and intuitive customer experience.

Identity theft protection services are often just marketing companies who slapped together identity theft protection with no basic knowledge of identity security. These companies create a hook to lure you in to buy their service, which they offer for around $100 to $200 per year. What they don't tell you is that their service doesn't do much more than scan the Internet looking for your data, and if your identity is stolen, they will only provide you some advice on how to fix it. Essentially, they are hedging their bets that only a few of their clients will actually become victims of identity theft. While they may do their best to fix your identity if it is stolen, this isn't protection you can count on.

Credit card companies, banks, and insurance companies all offer forms of identity protection. Many of them are white label services, rebranded to look as if they come from an entity with which you already do business. These services provide little or no value.

When you invest in identity theft protection, don't invest in a gimmicky marketing ploy that spends most of your monthly fee on advertising. You want a solid security company protecting you, and a solid security company handling your data.

#82: Do I Really Need Identity Theft Protection?

If you have seen advertisements for identity theft protection but assumed your identity would never be compromised and that protection is an unnecessary expense, I hope I have opened your eyes to the reality of the 21st century. We all need identity theft protection!

If you answer, "Yes" to any of the following questions and you don't have identity theft protection, you are at risk:

- Do you have a Social Security Number?
- Does your child have a Social Security Number?
- Do you have bills in your name? (This includes credit cards, loans, utilities, a cell phone, and so on.)
- Do you go to a doctor or dentist?

- Have you ever been admitted into a hospital?
- Do you have a driver's license?
- Do you file income taxes?
- Do you attend college or any form of higher education?
- Do you use the Internet?
- Do you never use the Internet?
- Do you have a bank account?
- Do you have no money?
- Do you have bad credit?
- Do you never use credit cards?
- Are you alive?

You get my point; unless you are dead, or live in the woods and have never checked into society, or were never documented by a government agency, or live without utilities and provide your own medical and dental services, you are at risk. Even homeless people are potential victims.

#83: What Is a Credit Freeze?

A credit freeze, or security freeze, locks down a person's credit file so that a potential lender can't check that person's credit. This is a good way to prevent a criminal from opening a new account under your name or using your Social

Security Number. If a creditor can't check your credit, they are less likely to extend credit to you or an identity thief.

For this important layer of security to be effective, you'll need a credit freeze from each of the three credit bureaus. The process of freezing your credit generally involves an affidavit with your name, address, Social Security Number, and a copy of a utility bill to verify your identity. Fees can be up to $15 per credit bureau.

Once this is complete, your identity, as far as new account fraud is concerned, is locked down pretty securely. Don't forget, though, that additional steps must be taken to ensure that your existing accounts and identity stay safe.

#84: What Is Credit Monitoring?

Credit monitoring is only available as an ongoing subscription service, often through an identity theft protection provider.

There are three credit bureaus that keep an ongoing account of your credit history—good and bad. Most people do not check their credit files and associated credit scores until they apply for credit and are turned down for some unanticipated reason.

Credit monitoring ensures that at least one, or preferably all three of your files at the various credit bureaus are monitored regularly, so that any unusual or unknown activity is discovered and reported back to you in a timely manner.

Credit monitoring informs when a lender requests your credit file and alerts you to possible fraud. If you have not applied for a loan or credit card, it is then your responsibility to act, contacting either the identity theft service provider or the creditor in question to refute the new account.

#85: What Is a Fraud Alert?

A fraud alert is a service that can be obtained through any of the three credit bureaus. It adds an additional layer of required authentication to the credit application process. If you or someone else applies for credit in your name while you have an active fraud alert, the lender or creditor will be prompted to verify your identification before extending a line of credit.

Fraud alerts are temporary, expiring after 90 days. While a fraud alert is a good tool, it is too temporary to consider it a viable long-term identity theft protection strategy.

If your identity has already been compromised, you can add an Extended Fraud Victim Alert to your report. To do this, you must submit a copy of a valid identity theft report that you filed with a federal, state, or local law enforcement agency. An Extended Alert will remain active for seven years.

If you are an active member of the military, you can request to add an Active Duty Alert to your credit report. An Active Duty Alert will remain on your file for one year.

#86: How Do I Protect My Child from Identity Theft?

Some would tell you, "Protect your child's Social Security Number." This is decent advice, but it is not practical as it is essentially impossible.

The best solution is to invest in identity theft protection for your child.

If you ever determine that your child's identity has been stolen, you should immediately file a report with your local police department. A police report is typically the first step in removing unauthorized accounts from the child's credit report.

TransUnion offers an online form to search for your child's information which can be found at transunion.com/corporate/personal/fraudIdentityTheft/fraudPrevention/childIDInquiry.page.

After submitting the completed form, you will be notified as to whether there is indeed a credit file linked to your child's identity, or if such a report does not yet exist. If there is no credit file associated with your child's name or Social Security Number, then your child's identity should be safe, at least as far as financial identity theft is concerned. If the response confirms that a credit file does exist for your child, you should immediately contact all three credit bureaus— TransUnion, Experian and Equifax—with your concerns.

You can request a free credit report for a child over the age of fourteen from www.annual-creditreport.com. If your child's identity has been used to open unauthorized accounts, you should contact local police and the credit bureaus.

#87: How Do I Protect Myself from Medical Identity Theft?

The Health Insurance Portability and Accountability Act, or HIPAA, was enacted in 1996 to help protect both the privacy of our medical records and our medical identities when our information is shared with health care providers, health plans, and other entities. HIPAA mandates that individuals be notified of any breaches of their medical information.

Most states require corporations to disclose data breaches. Since health care facilities often handle and store some of the same sensitive personal information that corporations do, these facilities are subject to similar regulations. However, protecting yourself from medical identity theft isn't as easy as protecting yourself from financial identity theft. Medical identification cards, insurance cards, and medical statements that come in the mail can be used to steal your medical identity.

To protect yourself from medical identity theft:

- Install a locking mailbox to prevent your mail from being stolen.
- Don't carry insurance or medical cards in your wallet unless it is absolutely necessary, such as when you have an actual appointment.
- Protect medical information documents. Shred all documentation prior to throwing it away and lock up files stored in your home or office.
- Obtain identity theft protection. If the thief can't steal your financial identity, then your medical identity may be less attractive.

Get a copy of your medical records from the Medical Information Bureau at www.MIB.com.

#88: How Do I Protect Myself from Criminal Identity Theft?

Other than by making your best effort to protect your identifying information, there is no guaranteed method to prevent your identity from being used by a criminal.

If you suspect someone may have used your information to commit a crime, you should conduct a background search on yourself, either through online databases available for most states, or by hiring a private investigator. Each state has some form of government-administered Criminal Offender Record Information bureau that catalogs criminal records. There are also paid search websites that will alert you to any possible criminal activity associated with your identity.

#89: How Do I Protect Myself from Identity Cloning?

Victims of identity cloning may or may not be adversely affected. They may never even know they have been cloned, but if they do find out, it may happen when bill collectors contact them, incorrect information appears on credit reports or tax returns, or, in a worst-case scenario, they may be arrested for crimes they did not commit.

The best form of protection encompasses all the previously described advice. Remember, identity cloning combines all forms of identity theft, so the more aware you are of your identity's health, and the more systems and precautions you have in place to monitor and lock down your identity, the more difficult it will be for a thief to pose as you.

#90: How Do I Protect Myself from Business or Commercial Identity Theft?

Business identity theft, or commercial identity theft, is often perpetrated from within a business or other organization. Company employees often have access to documents that include owners' and board members' Social Security Numbers, as well as the business' Tax ID number. It is imperative that this information stays secure.

Organizations should put a check and balance system into place, ensuring that for every employee who has access to company accounts, there are two employees—preferably upper management—who are assigned to make sure the books are balanced, that no money is missing, and that financial statements are double-checked for inaccuracies. In some instances, it is necessary to contract forensic accountants or examiners to pay close attention to a business' books and work to put monitoring systems in place.

Identity theft protection with credit monitoring can be a helpful tool to keep officers or owners informed of potential illicit activities, because a Social Security Number is often required to open accounts under a business's name.

CHAPTER 11

MORE ON PREVENTING IDENTITY THEFT AND RESTORING IT IF IT'S STOLEN

Identity theft is both an online and offline issue; it happens on the Internet and in the real world. Therefore, you must apply multiple layers of protection for your computer and for yourself. This is especially necessary since today, more than ever, our real-world identities and virtual identities are merging together.

#91: What Is the Best Way to Protect Myself from Identity Theft on Social Networks?

Facebook is the most popular social networking website, and consequently, a major target for cybercriminal activity. Facebook has recently taken on more accountability for users' security.

There are some precautions you should take when using a social networking website:

- Make sure to create a strong password that is at least eight characters in length and contains a combination of upper and lower case letters, numbers, and, if possible, symbols. Do not use the same password for all of your online accounts.
- Limit the information you post about yourself, and never provide your home address, employer's address, full date of birth, or detailed family information.
- Regularly check your privacy settings on social networks. Make sure that your personal information is only visible to your real-life friends and do not allow your information to be shared with third parties.

- Do not accept friend requests from people you don't know in the real word.
- Be aware of all the information you make available online, and consider everything you post as being visible to the public, even if you are using the strongest privacy settings available.

#92: How Do I Create a Secure Password?

There is no such thing as a truly secure password. There are only more secure or less secure passwords. Passwords are currently the most convenient and effective way to control access to your accounts.

Most people aren't aware of the numerous common techniques for cracking passwords:

- **Dictionary attacks:** There are free online tools that make password cracking almost effortless. Dictionary attacks rely on software that automatically plugs common words into password fields. So, don't use dictionary words, slang terms, common misspellings, or words spelled backward. Avoid consecutive keyboard combinations such as **qwerty** or **asdfg**.

165

- **Cracking security questions:** When you click the "Forgot Password" link within a webmail service or other website, you're asked to answer a question or series of questions to verify your identity. Many people use names of spouses, kids, other relatives, or pets in security questions or as passwords themselves. These types of answers can be deduced with a little research, and can often be found on your social media profile. Don't use traceable personal information in your security questions or passwords.

- **Simple passwords:** When 32 million passwords were exposed in a breach last year, almost 1 percent of victims were using **123456**. The next most popular password was **12345**. Other common choices are **111111**, **princess**, **qwerty**, and **abc123**. Avoid these types of passwords, which are easily guessed.

- **Reuse of passwords across multiple sites:** When one data breach compromises passwords, that same login information can often be used to hack into users' other accounts. Two recent breaches revealed a password reuse rate of 31 percent among victims. Reusing passwords for email, banking, and social media accounts can lead to identity theft.

- **Social engineering:** As previously described, social engineering is the act of manipulating others into performing certain actions or divulging confidential information, and can be used as an alternative to traditional hacking. Social engineering can be employed to trick targets into disclosing passwords.

One day we will develop a truly secure password, perhaps a cross-pollination of various access control tools such as biometrics, dynamic-based biometrics, image-based access, and multi-factor authentication. In the meantime, protect your information by creating a secure password that makes sense to you, but not to others.

Here are 15 more tips for making your password less vulnerable:

- Use different passwords for each of your accounts.
- Be sure no one watches as you enter your password.
- Always log off if there are other people in the vicinity of your laptop or other

device. It only takes a moment for someone to steal or change your password.

- Use comprehensive security software and keep it up to date to avoid keystroke log-gers and other malware.

- Avoid entering passwords on computers you don't control, such as at an Internet café or library. These computers may have malware that steals passwords.

- Avoid entering passwords when using unsecured Wi-Fi connections, such as at an airport or in a coffee shop. Hackers can intercept your passwords and other data over this unsecured connection.

- Don't share your password with anyone. Someone you trust right now might not be your friend in the future. Keep your passwords safe by keeping them to yourself.

- Depending on the sensitivity of the infor-mation being protected, you should change your passwords periodically and avoid reusing your previous password for at least one year.

- Use at least eight characters of upper and lowercase letters, numbers, and, if possi-ble, symbols in your password.

- Strong passwords are easy to remember but hard to guess. **Iam:)2b29!** has ten characters and says, "I am happy to be 29!" (I wish.)

- Use the keyboard as a palette to create shapes. Follow **%tgbHU8*-** on your keyboard. It's a V-shape, starting with any of the top keys. To change these periodically, you can slide the V across the keyboard. Use a W-shape if you are feeling crazy.

- Have fun with known short codes, sentences or phrases. E.g., **2B-or-Not_2b?** is **To be or not to be?**

- It's okay to write down your passwords, but keep them away from your computer, mixed in with other numbers and letters, so it's not apparent that they are passwords.

- Write down a clue to help you remember your password, but that doesn't actually include your password itself. In the example above, your clue might be, "To be, or not to be?"

- Check your password strength. If the website you are joining offers a password strength analyzer, pay attention to it and heed its advice.

#93: How Often Should I Review My Financial Statements, Credit Card Statements and Credit Reports?

Credit reports should be reviewed once every three months, at a minimum. If you have identity theft protection that includes credit monitoring, you can limit your review to semiannually. If your identity theft protection service offers unlimited credit reports, then check as often as you like, preferably monthly.

I check my bank's financial statements and credit card statements online at least once every two weeks. If you have the time to check daily, however, do it.

Credit cards offer some measure of protection when it comes to zero liability policies, as long as the cardholder refutes an unauthorized charge within 60 days. When a debit card is compromised, the stolen money can be more difficult to get back.

Federal laws limit credit cardholder liability to $50 in the case of credit card fraud, as long as the cardholder disputes the charge within 60 days. If a victim doesn't discover or report the fraud until after two billing cycles have passed, the liability could be the entire card balance. Once your debit card has been compromised, you might not find out until a check bounces or the card is declined. And once you do recover the funds, the thief can just start all over again, unless you cancel the account altogether.

In order to maintain the $50 liability limit, debit card fraud victims must notify the bank within two days of discovering the fraudulent transactions. After that, the maximum liability jumps to $500.

This falls under Federal Regulation E:[21]

"A consumer's liability for an unauthorized electronic fund transfer or a series of related unauthorized transfers shall be determined as follows:

(1) Timely notice given. If the consumer notifies the financial institution within two business days after learning of the loss or theft of the access

---

[21] "FDIC Laws, Regulations, Related Acts," Federal Deposit Insurance Corporation, last modified December 10, 2010,
http://www.fdic.gov/regulations/laws/rules/6500-3100.html.

device, the consumer's liability shall not exceed the lesser of $50 or the amount of unauthorized transfers that occur before notice to the financial institution.

(2) Timely notice not given. If the consumer fails to notify the financial institution within two business days after learning of the loss or theft of the access device, the consumer's liability shall not exceed the lesser of $500 or the sum of:

(i) $50 or the amount of unauthorized transfers that occur within the two business days, whichever is less."

#94: How Do I Protect Myself from New Account Fraud?

Follow the protection advice mentioned in this book, including measures that protect both your computer and your identity, such as credit freezes and fraud alerts.

You should also consider purchasing identity theft protection that monitors your credit for credit checks that are initiated prior to the opening of new accounts. Ensure that your protection provider also monitors the Internet for information that identity thieves can use to open accounts.

Without this window into your credit activity, you won't know that new accounts have been opened until it is too late.

#95: How Do I Protect Myself from Account Takeover Fraud?

Victims are often the first to detect account takeover after they discover unauthorized charges on a monthly statement or find that funds have been depleted from existing accounts. Check your financial and credit card statements frequently and monitor your credit reports. Follow the other advice mentioned in this book, including taking measures that protect both your computer and your identity, such as credit freezes and fraud alerts. You should also consider subscribing to an identity theft protection service.

#96: How Do I Protect Myself from Credit or Debit Card Fraud?

This is a form of account takeover. Follow the advice above, in "#94: How Do I Protect Myself from New Account Fraud" and "#95: How Do I Protect Myself from Account Takeover Fraud."

In particular, review online statements frequently and refute unauthorized charges immediately.

- Avoid using a debit card for everyday transactions
- Use credit cards and check charges online frequently. At a minimum, you should check statements bi-weekly—at least once a week but preferably once a day.
- Refute unauthorized charges immediately
- Follow the protection tips for online shopping security and protecting your computer.

#97: How Do I Protect Myself from Affinity Fraud?

The U.S. Securities and Exchange Commission provides the following recommendations:

- Check out everything, no matter how trustworthy the person seems who brings the investment opportunity to your attention. Never make an investment based solely on the recommendation of a member of an organization or religious or ethnic group to which you belong. Investigate the investment thoroughly and check the truth of every statement you are told about the investment. Be aware that the person telling you about the investment may have been fooled into believing that the investment is legitimate when it is not.

- Do not fall for investments that promise spectacular profits or *guaranteed* returns. If an investment seems too good to be true, then it probably is. Similarly, be extremely leery of any investment that is said to have no risks; very few investments are risk-free. The greater the potential return from an investment, the greater your risk of losing money. Promises of fast and high profits, with little or no risk, are classic warning signs of fraud.

- Be skeptical of any investment opportunity that is not in writing. Fraudsters often avoid putting things in writing, but legitimate investments are usually in writing. Avoid an investment if you are told they do "not have the time to reduce to writing" the particulars about the investment. You should also be suspicious if you are told to keep the investment opportunity confidential.

- Don't be pressured or rushed into buying an investment before you have a chance to think about—or investigate—the "opportunity." Just because someone you know made money, or claims to have made money, doesn't mean you will too. Be especially skeptical of investments that are pitched as "once-in-a-lifetime" opportunities, particularly when the promoter bases the recommendation on "inside" or confidential information.

Fraudsters are increasingly using the Internet to target particular groups through e-mail spam. If you receive an unsolicited e-mail from someone you don't know, containing a "can't miss" investment, your best move is to pass up the "opportunity" and forward the spam to us at enforcement@sec.gov.[22]

#98: How Do I Restore My Identity Once It Has Been Stolen?

The Federal Trade Commission offers invaluable tools for restoring your identity if it has already

---

[22] "Affinity Fraud," SEC (see chap. 3, n. 15).

been compromised. The tools can be found at
www.ftc.gov/bcp/edu/microsites/idtheft/tools.html.
On this website, you will find a complaint form,
affidavit of your identity, and sample letters.
You will also find a log to chart your actions
while restoring your identity. It is important to
utilize this log to keep a record of contacts you
have made with the authorities, credit card companies, banks, and credit bureaus. If something
gets lost in the process, the log ensures detailed
notes to help prove your efforts, and ultimately,
rescue your identity from a criminal.

If you have an all-encompassing identity theft
protection service, your provider can take care of
much of the restoration.

The first call you make should be to the police,
to report the crime. According to the FTC, "A
police report that provides specific details of the
identity theft is considered an Identity Theft
Report, which entitles you to certain legal rights
when it is provided to the three major credit
reporting agencies or to companies where the
thief misused your information. An Identity
Theft Report can be used to permanently block
fraudulent information that results from identity
theft, such as accounts or addresses, from

appearing on your credit report. It will also make sure these debts do not reappear on your credit reports. Identity Theft Reports can prevent a company from continuing to collect debts that result from identity theft, or selling them to others for collection. An Identity Theft Report is also needed to place an extended fraud alert on your credit report."[23]

When filing an identity theft report, you will first want to fill out an ID Theft Complaint (http://www.ftc.gov/bcp/edu/microsites/idtheft/consumers/filing-a-report.html) with the FTC, which you should bring with you to the police station.

If you are a victim of account takeover fraud, an Identity Theft Report may not be necessary. As long as the fraudulent charges are discovered in a timely manner, you can dispute the charges with your financial institution and, typically, have them removed. You should still file a police

---

[23] "About Identity Theft," Fighting Back Against Identity Theft: Federal Trade Commission, accessed May 11, 2011, http://www.ftc.gov/bcp/edu/microsites/idtheft/consumers/about-identity-theft.html#Whatcanyoudotohelpfightidentitytheft.

report to document the crime if you experience roadblocks in your efforts to have the charges removed. A police report will also be required to gain access to any credit applications the criminal may have completed, as well as to dispute charges that were made to accounts that you did not open. It may be discouraging because, in some instances, you may find that you are barred from accessing this information because the *thief's* privacy is protected.

The second step is to contact the three major credit bureaus and any creditors, such as banks or financial institutions. Inform them of the situation and put a freeze or a fraud alert on your accounts and credit reports.

The FTC website listed above provides regularly updated information on the steps necessary to regain your life.

The Office of Consumer Affairs and Business Regulation in Massachusetts outlines guidelines that are similar to those provided by other states and federal agencies, and suggests the following steps when responding to a potential identity theft:

Contact your creditors and banks immediately: These creditors may include credit card companies, banks, utility companies, and even landlords. Once you obtain the names and telephone numbers of the creditors whose accounts appear on your report as the result of fraud, contact them by telephone and in writing. Let them know about the fraud, and ask for a copy of all account information and, if applicable, the credit application. Be prepared to fill out affidavits of forgery to establish your innocence.

You should also get replacement cards, new account numbers, and passwords for all of your legitimate accounts. Ask the creditors to issue a unique password for your account that is not associated with your Social Security Number or your mother's maiden name.

If checking accounts have been fraudulently established under your name, file a report with the following check verification companies:

- CheckRite: (800) 780-2305
- ChexSystems: (800) 428-9623
- SCAN: (800) 262-7771
- Telecheck: (800) 710-9898

Begin keeping records: Start a log of the time and money you spend correcting your credit history. Under recently enacted state and federal law, any person found guilty of financial identity theft will be ordered to pay restitution to the victim for any financial loss, including lost wages and attorney's fees. Your records will help document your losses. In addition, some identity theft victims have experienced difficulty in cleaning up their credit histories and have found it necessary to take legal action against creditors and credit reporting agencies. This log should document your efforts to communicate and resolve the problems. Your log should include every phone conversation, including the date and time of your call, and the name and title of the person who assisted you. You should confirm all phone conversations in writing and keep copies of these letters and any other documents you send or receive.

Flag your credit file for fraud: Call the fraud departments of the three major credit reporting agencies listed below:

- Equifax: (888) 766-0008
- Experian: (888) 397-3742
- TransUnion: (800) 680-7289

Request your credit report be flagged with a fraud alert and add to your report a statement that you are a victim of fraud and that all creditors should contact you at a phone number you provide to verify all future applications. Each of the major credit bureaus may have different procedures, so ask each one how long the fraud alert will remain on your report and the circumstances under which that period may be extended. You should also request a written copy of your report to review and verify that each piece of credit information is valid.

Warning: Placing a fraud alert may not necessarily prevent the fraud from resuming. Some creditors may not see these alerts if they do not obtain your full consumer report, but rather rely on a credit score or another automated credit application system. You will need to continue monitoring your report. Ask the credit bureau if they will supply you with a free copy every few months.

Review your credit reports: Look for credit accounts that you did not create and public records information that is incorrect and should not be linked to you, such as a court judgment. The credit bureau will be able to provide you with the full names, addresses, and phone numbers of the creditors with whom the identity thief opened accounts.

To have these fraudulent accounts taken off your report, you will need to write a letter to the credit bureau formally disputing these accounts. The credit bureau will have 30 days to investigate and remove any erroneous or unverified information.

You should also review your credit report for companies that have inquired about your credit without your approval. Ask the credit bureau to remove inquiries that are the result of fraud. Too many inquiries on your credit report within a short period of time may result in your denial of credit.

Report the crime: You should report incidents of identity theft to the appropriate authorities, depending on the nature of the crime.

- **Police:** File a police report and criminal complaint with your local police department and/or district attorney's office. Theft of financial identity is a criminal act in Massachusetts punishable by a fine of up to $5,000 and/or up to two and a half years in jail and restitution of financial loss to the victim. In addition, law enforcement may use the federal Identity Theft and Assumption Deterrence Act of 1998 to prosecute identity imposters. Be sure to keep a copy of your filed complaint, as some creditors may request it for verification of your case.

- **Federal Trade Commission (FTC)**: The FTC is the federal clearinghouse for complaints by victims of identity theft. Although the FTC does not have the authority to bring criminal cases, it assists victims by providing them with information to help them resolve the problems that can result from identity theft. You may call the FTC toll-free at 877-ID-THEFT (438-4338), or log on to: www.consumer.gov/idtheft.

- **Secret Service:** The Financial Crimes Division is charged with investigating crimes associated with financial institutions. Typically, it will track complaints in an effort to discover crime rings, but will not investigate individual complaints. You can contact the Massachusetts Regional Office at 10

Causeway Street, Boston, MA 02222-1080, 617-565-5640.

- **U.S. Postal Inspector:** Postal Inspectors may have jurisdiction over your case if the identity thief has used the mail to commit credit or bank fraud.

  If you can determine where the fraudulent credit cards or checks were sent, contact the local postmaster for that address and to file a complaint. Be sure to request that change of address forms submitted on your behalf not be accepted.

- **The Federal Bureau of Investigation:** The FBI also may investigate financial crimes. Typically, the FBI focuses on fraud rings engaged in conspiracies to defraud financial institutions. You can contact the Massachusetts Regional Office at Suite 600, One Center Plaza Boston, MA, 02108 (617) 742-5533.

- **Social Security Administration:** To report the fraudulent use of your Social Security Number, you should contact the Office of the Inspector General's Fraud Hotline at 1-800-269-0271 and follow-up in writing. Ask if you are eligible to change your Social Security Number. The Social Security Administration, however, cannot help individuals fix personal records at credit bureaus, credit card companies, or banks.

Address public record errors: Your credit report may include civil judgments entered in your name for illegal actions committed by your identity thief. If this has happened to you, contact the court where the judgment was rendered and provide them with documentation that you are an identity theft victim.

Public records information is tracked not only by the three major credit bureaus, but also by smaller services like tenant screening companies, check verification businesses, and individual reference services. Contact these services as well to ensure that any false judgments entered in your name are removed from their files.[24]

---

[24] "Surviving Theft of Financial Identity," Consumer Affairs and Business Regulation, accessed May 11, 2011, http://www.mass.gov/?pageID=ocaterminal&L=3&L0=Home&L1=Consumer&L2=Finance&sid=Eoca&b=terminalcontent&f=surviving_theft_of_financial_identity&csid=Eoca.

#99: How Long Will It Take to Restore My Identity?

This is a question that I am frequently asked, and is one of the most difficult to answer. The effects of identity theft can be a part of your life for hours, days, or even years. The specific type of identity theft that occurred and the level of damage that has been done are the major determining factors. There is also the possibility that the initial thief is not the only person who has your information.

Rogue websites can go up in a day and disappear even more quickly, with the sole purpose of exchanging the identifying information and credit card, debit card, and bank account numbers of unsuspecting, honest individuals. For this reason, diligent record-keeping and monitoring of your financial accounts will be necessary to regain your life. Immediately report anything that seems suspicious or inaccurate, because the longer the period of time that elapses between the initial criminal act and the moment you discover and report it, the more difficult it will be to remove the information from your records.

IN CONCLUSION

I did not write this book to scare you into purchasing identity theft protection or antivirus software, or to spend more money than you need to. My intention is to educate you on the methods, dangers, and implications of identity theft, and point you toward the tools you need to protect yourself.

Criminals are employing an increasing number of advanced technological tools to steal from their victims. You can't expect to protect yourself without the assistance of current technology and security services.

Through sharing stories of people like you and I who found themselves victims of identity theft and by informing you of the multitude of ways criminals can access your information, I hope I have brought a new level of awareness into your life, so that you will have the knowledge necessary to protect yourself and your family from identity thieves.

Do not sit around and worry about the threats outlined in this book. Worrying doesn't do any good. You need to act. You need to realize that there are criminals actively seeking their next target. You want to take precautions so that they do not choose you.

The first thing I tell the people who attend my seminars is, "The chances of anything bad ever happening to you are very slim. So don't worry about it. However, you should still put these systems into place."

I heard somewhere that 90 percent of what we worry about never happens. It might even be closer to 99 percent, but that remaining one percent is still a real concern.

If you knew the statistical probability of your child being shot at school, or being kidnapped, or struck by lightning, and in all three cases the odds were slim, would you take fewer precautions to protect yourself or your family? Would you stand next to a metal pole in a thunderstorm? Would you drive without a seatbelt? Would you allow your seven-year-old, who is perfectly capable of navigating his way to school, go alone, even though the odds of him being kidnapped are extremely slim?

Many of the issues we worry about might have a one in 100,000 or one in ten million chance of actually happening. The odds that something terrible will impact your life may roughly equate to the odds that you'll win the lottery, but people still play the lottery, right? Does it really matter what the odds are? Every day someone, somewhere, wins the lottery. And every day someone, somewhere, is a victim of identity theft.

In summary, knowing what I know, I'm concerned about the dangers, but I take the necessary steps to prevent what I can. Do I worry? I prefer to channel that energy into putting measures into place to prevent the bad things that could happen. If being proactive and taking responsibility are worrying, then yes, I do. However, I feel safe, secure, and grounded, without any nagging paranoia that detracts from my quality of life.

Stay safe,

Robert Siciliano
http://RobertSiciliano.com

APPENDIX A:

WORKSHEETS

Notes to Self:

Notes to Self:

Notes to Self:

Notes to Self:

Notes to Self:

Notes to Self:

APPENDIX B:

RESOURCES

Annual Credit Report—
www.annualcreditreport.com

Apple Security Updates—
support.apple.com/kb/HT1222

Equifax—
http://www.equifax.com/cs/Satellite?pagename=
contact_us

Experian—
http://www.experian.com/corporate/personal-
services-contacts.html

Federal Bureau of Investigation (FBI)—
Massachusetts Regional Office Suite 600, One
Center Plaza Boston, MA, 02108 (617) 742-5533

Federal Trade Commission (FTC)—
877-ID-THEFT (438-4338) or
http://www.ftc.gov/ or
www.consumer.gov/idtheft

Identity Theft Resource Center—
http://www.idtheftcenter.org/

Javelin Research & Strategy—
https://www.javelinstrategy.com/

McAfee—
http://www.mcafee.com/us/

McAfee Cybersafety Resource Portal—
www.mcafee.com/cru

McAfee Security Advice Center—
www.mcafee.com/advice

Medical Information Bureau—
www.MIB.com

Microsoft Security Update—
http://www.update.microsoft.com/

Robert Siciliano—
http://RobertSiciliano.com

Privacy Rights Clearinghouse—
https://www.privacyrights.org/

Secret Service—
Financial Crimes Division Massachusetts
Regional Office at 10 Causeway Street, Boston,
MA 02222-1080, 617-565-5640

Social Security Administration—
Office of the Inspector General's Fraud Hotline
at 1-800-269-0271

STOP. THINK. CONNECT. —
http://www.stopthinkconnect.org/

TransUnion—
http://www.transunion.com/corporate/personal/c
onsumerSupport/contactUs.page

Wi-Fi Protected Access—
http://www.wi-fi.org/knowledge_center/wpa2

Phone Listings

CheckRite: (800) 780-2305

ChexSystems: (800) 428-9623

Equifax: (888) 766-0008

Experian: (888) 397-3742

SCAN: (800) 262-7771

Telecheck: (800) 710-9898

TransUnion: (800) 680-7289

ABOUT THE AUTHOR

ROBERT SICILIANO

ROBERT SICILIANO, CEO of IDTheftSecurity.com, is fiercely committed to informing, educating, and empowering Americans so they will be better able to protect themselves from violence and crime in the physical and virtual worlds. His "tell it like it is" style is sought after by major media outlets, executives of leading corporations, meeting planners, and community leaders who seek the straight talk they need to stay safe in a world where physical and virtual crime is common-place. Siciliano is accessible, real, professional, and ready to weigh in and comment on breaking news at a moment's notice.

His goal is simple—to wake up and empower people across Main Street, USA, so they can avoid being victims of crime. His personal security and identity theft expertise are assets to any program or organization that demands straight talk, common sense, and potentially life and property saving results right now. Whether he is speaking on camera, to a reporter, or sharing his identity theft and personal security stories and tips as a keynote speaker or workshop leader, Siciliano's direct and to-the-point tone of voice can be counted on to capture attention, and, most importantly, inspire and empower action.

He wants people everywhere to do the right things to keep family, data, and property safe. Audience members describe his credible, from-the-trenches advice as life-changing and life-saving.

Siciliano's media credentials include hard-hitting and provocative contributions to *The Today Show, CBS Early Show, CNN, MSNBC, CNBC, Fox News, Inside Edition, EXTRA, The Tyra Banks Show, Sally Jessy Raphael, The Montel Williams Show, The Maury Povich Show, Howard Stern, The Wall Street Journal, USA Today, Forbes, BusinessWeek, Cosmopolitan, Good Housekeeping, Reader's Digest, Consumer*

Digest, Smart Money, The New York Times, The Washington Post, and many more.

In addition to his role as a frequently quoted television news correspondent, Siciliano is the author of "The Safety Minute: Living on High Alert–How to Take Control of Your Personal Security and Prevent Fraud." Chief Executive Officers, Chief Information Officers, and Boards of Directors from leading corporations such as McAfee, iovation, Intelius, ADT, Gemalto, RSA, Sentry Safe, and Uni-Ball Corporation rely upon Siciliano's insights, perspectives, and guidance to bring additional firepower and protections to their system and customer security initiatives.

Siciliano consumes at least three hours of media each day. He subscribes to over 500 RSS feeds and monitors over 100 Google Alerts to stay up to speed and in the know about all matters relating to personal and information security. "I'm always on top of what is new and ahead of what is next with respect to all things personal security," Siciliano says.

Along his 29-year career path, he's studied martial arts, self-defense, human behavior, white-collar crime, cybercrime, and identity theft. He's even worked as a barroom bouncer and a personal bodyguard. His lifelong interest in these subjects is an asset to those who engage with and benefit from his expertise.

Security is a wide-ranging topic of great depth. Siciliano discusses all aspects of security as they relate to violence and fraud prevention in both the physical and virtual worlds. He can show you how to keep home invaders from assaulting you and taking your family hostage or keep criminal hackers from accessing your network and downloading client data. He provides topical, timely and cutting-edge programs to suit your group's wants and needs.

Contact Robert Siciliano at <u>RobertSiciliano.com</u>.

Available Titles in the 99 Series®

www.99-Series.com

CPSIA information can be obtained at www.ICGtesting.com
Printed in the USA
LVOW060425141212

311615LV00001B/11/P